DISCOVER Aerodynamics with Paper Airplanes

Written and Illustrated by
Norman Schmidt

Peguis Publishers

CONTENTS

PART ONE
Solving the mystery of flight   *1*

PART TWO
Basic aerodynamics   *7*
    Moving air creates lift   *8*
    Moving air gives control   *12*
    Moving air and airplane shape   *15*

PART THREE
Experimental flight   *21*
    Experiment 1: Principles into practice   *21*
    Experiment 2: Basic controls   *21*
    Experiment 3: Airplane performance   *24*
    Experiment 4: Competition flying   *29*

Glossary of terms   *39*

Reproducible airplane plans   *41*

© 1991, Norman Schmidt.

All rights reserved. Except as noted, no part of this book may be reproduced or transmitted in any form by any means without written permission of the publisher.

Designed and illustrated by Norman Schmidt.
Cover photo by Mike Maskell. Photos in the book by Paul Martens.
Printed and bound in Canada by Hignell Printing Limited.

91   92   93   94   95   5   4   3   2   1

Canadian Cataloguing in Publication Data

Schmidt, Norman Jacob, 1947-
Discover aerodynamics with paper airplanes

ISBN 0-920541-43-7

1. Aerodynamics – Study and teaching (Secondary) – Audio-visual aids.   2. Aerodynamics – Problems, exercises, etc.   3. Paper Airplanes.   I. Title.

TL573.S346 1991   629.132/3/0078   C91-097088-2

Peguis Publishers Limited
520 Hargrave Street
Winnipeg MB Canada R3A 0X8

The graceful flight of birds has inspired many a would-be human flyer. Here is a duck coming in for a landing. Notice the angle of its wings and body, which are used as air brakes.

PART ONE

SOLVING THE MYSTERY OF FLIGHT

AVE YOU EVER WONDERED how it is that such big and heavy objects as airplanes can be made to fly through the air? They seem to fly with such ease. Maybe you dream about flying.

For a long time people have wished that they could fly. They wondered about the relationship between air and solid objects. They saw leaves being swept from the trees as autumn winds blew in gusts, carrying them along in a haphazard sort of way. They saw strong winds blow down big trees and even rip roofs from houses and carry them great distances. They also saw birds flying through the air in a controlled manner, taking off and landing gracefully. Birds inspired them.

An ancient Greek story tells of Daedalus and his son Icarus who wanted to fly across the ocean. So Daedalus made wings of bird feathers held together with wax. He warned his son not to fly too high or the heat from the sun would melt the wax. But Icarus did not listen. He got carried away and flew so high that the wax melted. The feathers dropped from his wings and he fell to his death. But the story is a dream story – a myth.

People did not actually understand the effects of moving air on solid objects. They did not know what it was about air that made flying possible. Flying was a mystery. Even though they tried to fly, they were not successful in their attempts. For many years all they could do was wish.

But people were curious about flight and kept looking at birds, the air, and solid objects, hoping to discover something that might give them the ability to fly. Their curiosity paid off. Several discoveries were made by different people over a period of many years that finally led to solving the mystery.

In the ancient myth, Icarus fell to his death when the wax holding together his wings melted and all the feathers fell off. Many early attempts at flight ended in disaster.

In the 1480s, in Italy, an artist and inventor by the name of Leonardo da Vinci began to look carefully at how birds fly. He thought that it should be possible for humans to provide power for flight, like they do for a bicycle. He observed that birds have many different shapes and do different things with their wings and tails as they fly. They twist and turn their wings and tails so that air is deflected in different directions, resulting in controlled flight. In building his machines, he wanted the same kind of control, so he imitated birds and made machines with moving wings that flapped. But he didn't know that birds are shaped and control the air in very specific ways. He did not know about air pressure differential and lift. In imitating birds he was on the right track. When his helper was killed trying to fly in one of his machines, however, Leonardo became discouraged. He gave up on the idea of flight altogether. Flying remained a mystery.

During the 1600s and 1700s scientists began to examine the earth and sky more closely, examining how solids and fluids interact. It was discovered that air is not the lightest substance on the face of the earth and that air itself is not always the same weight. Daniel Bernoulli, a Swiss mathematician who lived from 1700 to 1782, made a very important observation about fluids in motion. He found that the pressure of a fluid always decreases as its rate of flow (speed) increases. Today we call this Bernoulli's Principle. He discovered what Leonardo needed to know.

In 1783 two brothers, Jacques and Joseph Montgolfier, noticed that smoke always seemed to rise upward. They thought that if a substance lighter than air could be contained in a large hollow ball and attached to a basket that it would be lifted upward. They filled a bag with smoke and it rose into the air. They discovered that it was heat that made the smoke lighter than the rest of the air. After that they built many different hot air balloons that carried people high and far. Others built balloons filled with gases lighter than air, like hydrogen and helium. Balloons could only drift in the wind, however. Their direction could not be controlled. If the wind was blowing from the north and you happened to want to go east, a balloon was no good. Therefore their use for transportation was limited.

When steam engines were invented, they were almost immediately put to use in providing propulsion for balloons. In 1852, Henri Giffard built the first steam-driven balloon with a rudder so that he could control its direction of travel. These balloons, called dirigibles, were often cigar-shaped. Large dirigibles were used for carrying both passengers and freight to many countries around the world. The largest carried about fifty people and travelled at seventy nautical miles per hour. But even with engines, the lighter-than-air craft were difficult to maneuver because of their very large gas bags.

By observing the effects of wind, people had known since ancient times that moving air has the ability to move objects. Kite flying had long been a popular pastime but no one knew exactly how kites flew. It was not until the age of balloons that people began to experiment with different shapes of kites to improve their lift. Between the years of 1799 and 1806 the Englishman Sir George Cayley discovered how Bernoulli's principle could be practically applied to kites to improve the lifting effect of moving air. By observing where air pressure was high and low on a kite's surface, he could shape it to take advantage of high pressure points to increase lift. Baskets were attached to large kites so that people could be lifted into the sky. Once Cayley's discovery was made it was a small step to remove the string from a kite and make a free-flying gliding airplane. Cayley built many kites and small-scale gliders.

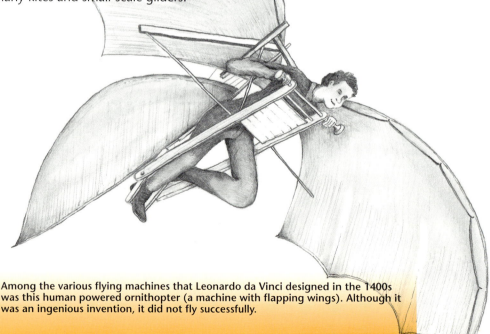

Among the various flying machines that Leonardo da Vinci designed in the 1400s was this human powered ornithopter (a machine with flapping wings). Although it was an ingenious invention, it did not fly successfully.

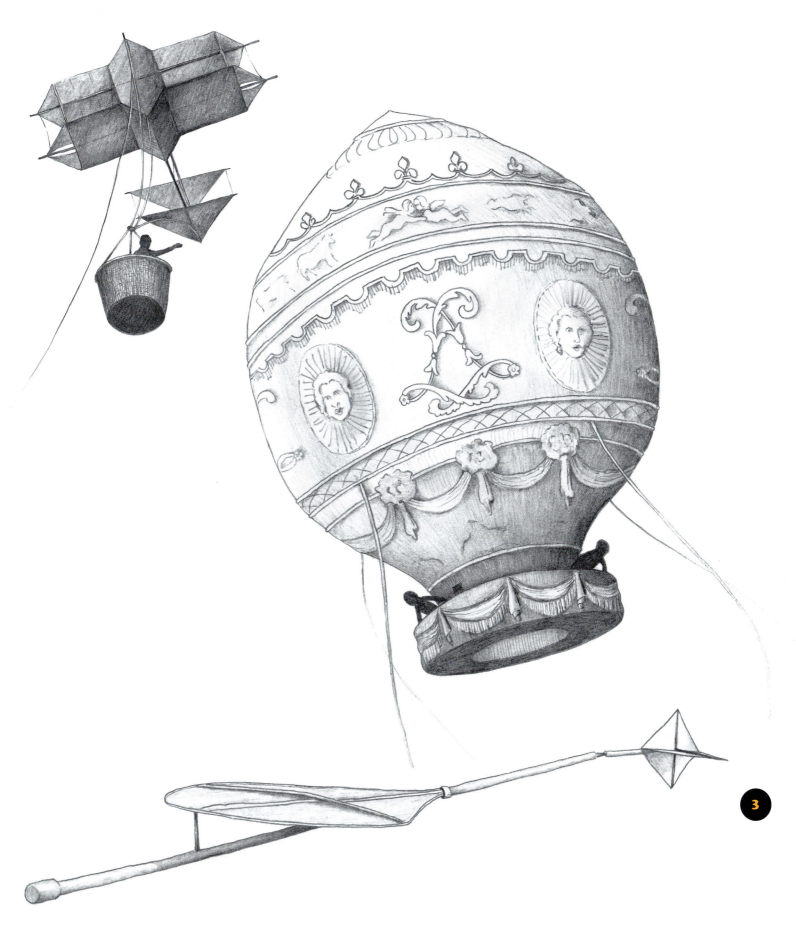

The first manned flight of a balloon took place in 1783 when two Frenchmen took to the air in a hot air balloon built by the Montgolfier brothers.

Flying kites has long been a favorite pastime. During the 1800s it became popular to build kites that were able to lift a person into the air.

Sir George Cayley, applying Bernoulli's Principle, built many kites and small-scale gliders with improved lift characteristics. In 1804 he built this model of a free-flying glider. It could not lift the weight of a person.

Otto Lilienthal, a German, was the first to build gliders that could carry his weight and that he could control in flight. He made many successful gliding flights during the 1880s before he met with a fatal crash one windy day. In his gliding flights he studied the lifting effect of moving air flowing across the wings and wrote down measurements of air pressure. Although his measurements later proved not to be very accurate, they served as a basis for further study.

Many individuals experimented with the problems of flight – most of them unsuccessfully. But in the United States, two brothers, Orville and Wilbur Wright, had success. They built testing devices to measure air pressure and were able to take much more accurate readings than Lilienthal had. With the invention of the gasoline engine, a lightweight source of power for propulsion became available. In 1903, with these advances, the brothers could remain airborne in powered and controlled flight. By 1905 they had made flights of more than 30 minutes covering distances of more than 25 kilometres. At long last, with the Wright brothers, the wish to control the air came true. The mystery had been solved and flying was a reality.

But many refinements followed. To build successful airplanes the shapes and lift characteristics of wings had to be properly synchronized with engine output. From the very beginning, airplane builders tried to see how fast and how far their machines could fly. In 1909 Louis Bleriot, a French airplane builder, crossed the open water of the English Channel. In 1912 Louis Bechereau, also French, was the first to fly at a speed of 100 nautical miles per hour. He flew the Deperdussin. Wing shapes and fuselages were developed that allowed for greater speed and better control. Engines became more reliable. As airplane design improved, the distances airplanes could fly without refuelling increased from a few hundred kilometers to several thousand. The 1920s saw great "flying boats" carry passengers across the vast oceans. By the 1940s, land-based airplanes crossed the ocean with ease. Finally the ancient attempts of Daedalus and Icarus were realized. Speeds increased steadily. During the 1930s racers passed the 300 nautical miles per hour mark, and by the end of the Second World War in 1945, speeds of almost 500 had been attained.

It was found that gasoline-burning piston engines could only produce so much power and no more. Hans von Ohain, a German scientist, and Frank Whittle, an English scientist, both tried to build a more powerful engine, one that did not depend on pistons but used a turbine and an air compressor. Who would succeed first? In the 1930s they both built successful prototype jet engines but war interrupted their research. They were on opposite sides. It was in 1944 that the first actual airplane using the jet engine for propulsion was built in Germany. Ohain had won, but this success came too late to affect the outcome of the war.

By the end of the 1950s many airplanes used jet engines as they do today. Speeds increased to more than the speed of sound. But there was a problem with increasing speed. Sound travels at about 700 nautical miles per hour. At that speed the flow of air across an airplane changes. It streams away from the surface. Even piston-driven airplanes could reach speeds approaching the speed of sound while in a dive that resulted in a loss of control. It was realized that for supersonic flight a different shape of airplane was needed. Nobody knew exactly how to build an airplane that would remain in control when it flew faster than the speed of sound. But it was known that certain bullets travelled faster than the speed of sound and remained in straight flight. The first supersonic airplane was built in the shape of a big bullet with short wings. In 1947 Chuck Yeager first flew the bullet-shaped Bell X-1 at supersonic speed.

But speed isn't everything. With present day jet engines the most efficient way to fly is below the speed of sound. Since the 1950s the average passenger airliner cruises at about 500 nautical miles per hour at an altitude of around 10,000 metres, just above most turbulent weather conditions.

However, supersonic speed has a place – in long distance flights and for military interceptors. Today the fastest passenger airplane is the Concorde, which flies at about twice the speed of sound. It takes only three hours to fly 100 passengers from North America to Europe.

Daedalus and Icarus would be impressed with today's air travel. In the future there will probably be airplanes that fly many times the speed of sound. For propulsion they will combine jet and rocket engines, and to avoid the great resistance of dense lower atmosphere air at high speed, will fly at the outer limits of the atmosphere. They will probably be able to fly halfway around the world in three hours. For slower flying airplanes there will be an increasing need to be more efficient and emit less pollutants. Airplane builders continue to experiment to this end.

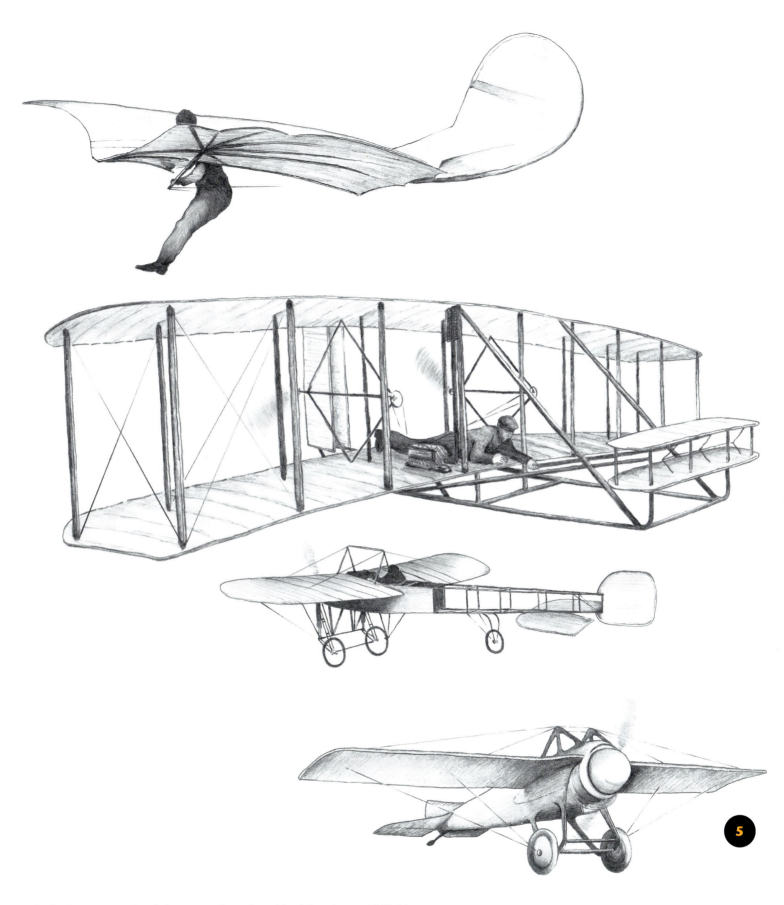

In the 1880s Otto Lilienthal was experimenting with gliders that could lift his weight and that he was able to control successfully while in flight.

After experimenting with gliders, the Wright brothers successfully flew an airplane called "The Flyer" under its own power in controlled flight for the first time in 1903.

In July of 1909 Louis Bleriot, testing his airplane's durability, was the first person to fly across the open water of the English Channel in his Number 11 airplane.

It was soon obvious that speed was natural to flight. The fastest airplane flying in 1912 was the Deperdussin. It was the first airplane to exceed 100 nautical miles per hour.

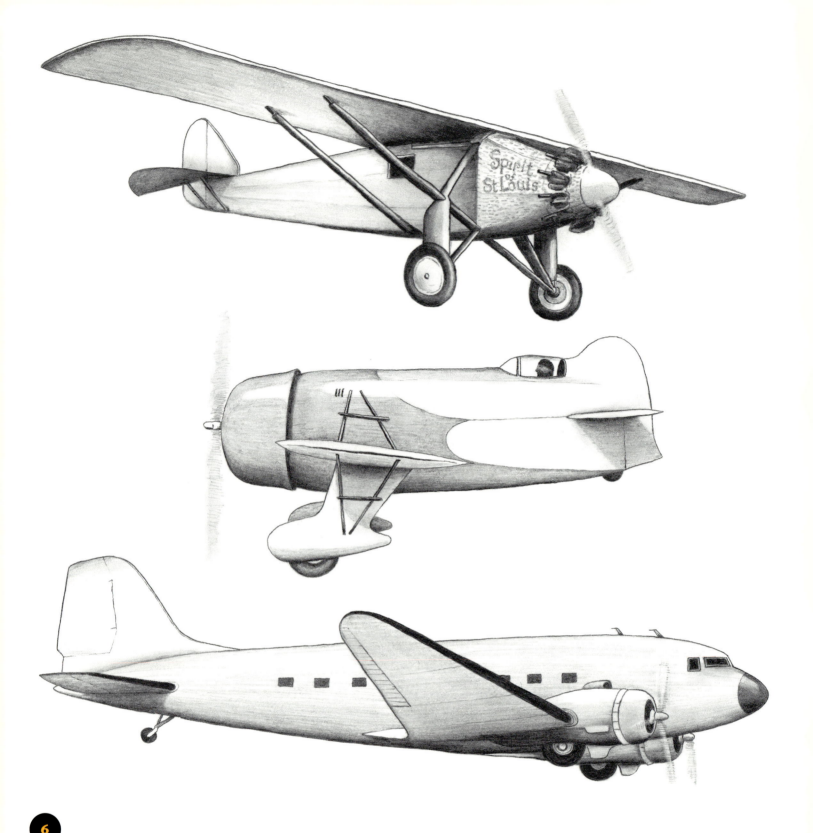

With a real sense of adventure Charles Lindbergh tested the durability of aircraft. He made the first non-stop solo flight across the Atlantic Ocean in the spring of 1927, flying this Ryan B1 called the "Spirit of St. Louis".

Setting speed records has always been popular among aviators. This strange looking racer called the "Gee Bee", was flown to almost 300 nautical miles per hour in 1932 by Jimmy Doolittle, one of the U.S.A.'s most famous flyers.

All the testing and racing resulted in ever greater dependability to be built into aircraft. The solidly built and aerodynamically sound Douglas DC3, designed in 1935, was the first passenger airplane to come into widespread use around the world. It has proven to be one of the most important airplanes to have been built because it popularized air travel everywhere. Many are still in use today.

PART TWO

BASIC AERODYNAMICS

IR IS AN INVISIBLE FLUID that exerts a great deal of force when it moves. Still air also exerts force. It presses on all sides of an object. If the object is motionless the AIR PRESSURE is even on all sides. This force presses on us, on our houses, our bicycles, and our airplanes – on everything. We are not usually aware of this pressure. Another force that is exerted on every object on the face of the earth is GRAVITY. Gravity pulls everything on the earth downward to the ground. The force with which gravity pulls downward gives us and all objects weight. If we throw something into the air, gravity pulls it back to the ground. When you ride your bike you feel the resistance of air as it flows across you. No matter how fast you go, gravity keeps you and your bike on the ground. But the faster you go the more the air resists.

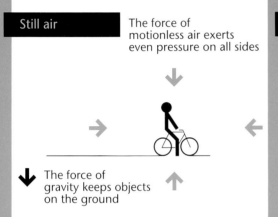

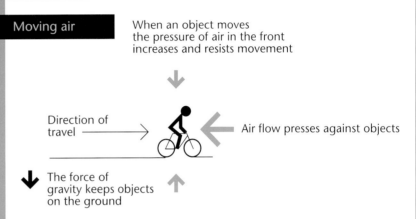

When an airplane moves forward it has four main forces acting upon it. An airplane's forward motion is maintained by the force of THRUST. With a paper airplane, thrust is initiated by the act of throwing. (The force of the engine provides thrust in a full-sized airplane.) As it moves forward, an airplane encounters resistance from the air (just like you do when you ride your bike fast) that tugs at its surfaces. This is called DRAG. As thrust drives it forward, an airplane's wings begin LIFTing it into the air, counteracting the force of GRAVITY that is always trying to pull it down to the ground (just like it does you and your bicycle). When a full-sized airplane takes off from the runway, its thrust must be great enough to accelerate and to counteract drag. The force of lift counteracts gravity as it speeds up and rises into the sky.

The first law of motion states that if an object is in equilibrium, it tends to remain so. There is no tendency for it to change its state or accelerate or decelerate. To continue moving forward straight and level in the air, thrust must equal drag and lift must equal the force of gravity. In accordance with the first law of motion, the four forces must be in exact balance. With a paper airplane, drag is always slightly more than thrust. It gently descends as the wings produce less and less lift and gravity pulls it down to the ground.

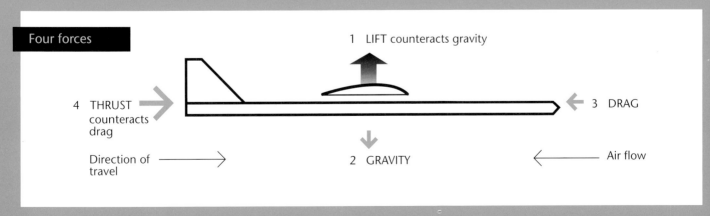

7

Moving air creates lift

Have you ever wondered why an airplane that is moving forward stays in the air and one that is motionless does not? A full-sized airplane is a heavy object that must somehow be lifted into the sky. The study of aerodynamics gives us some insight into the mystery of the flight of objects that are heavier than air. Both birds and airplanes fly according to the same principles.

THE KEY TO HEAVIER-THAN-AIR FLIGHT
Aerodynamics is the study of air as it moves around objects. It began with Daniel Bernoulli, a Swiss mathematician. His discovery led to an understanding of how birds fly and to the creation of heavier-than-air flying machines.

THINK AND DO:
You can demonstrate what Bernoulli discovered. Cut a strip of paper 3 cm wide and 15 cm long. Tape one of the narrow edges to a pencil. Hold the pencil so that the paper sticks out and slants down slightly away from you. Blow air through a drinking straw along the TOP of the paper from the taped end. What happens?

- *Does your blowing move the paper?*
- *In which direction does the paper move when you blow over its top?*
- *Does blowing harder make a difference?*
- *Why does the paper move in the direction it does? Do you think the force of the pressure UNDERNEATH the paper is greater or less than the force of the pressure of the moving air above it?*

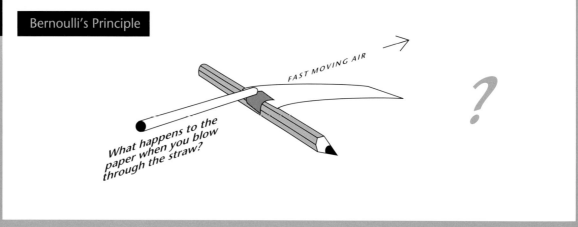

Bernoulli's Principle

Bernoulli discovered that THE PRESSURE OF A FLUID (AIR) ALWAYS DECREASES AS ITS SPEED INCREASES. We call this BERNOULLI'S PRINCIPLE. Therefore, if faster air has lower pressure, then slower air must have higher pressure. When you blow through the straw you speed up the flow of air which lowers its pressure, creating a difference of pressure above and below the paper.

SHAPE AND LIFT
When birds and airplanes fly, the pressure of the air above them is less than it is below so they are pushed upwards. How does a bird's wing make a differential of pressure to enable it to fly? How do we copy nature? When air flows across and around horizontal plane surfaces (wings) something important happens. As a wing moves forward it slices the air into two layers, one above and one below it, like a sandwich. As the wing moves, these two layers of air flow from front to back. The trick is for the top layer or stream of air to have lower pressure than the bottom one. This can be done by giving the wing a particular profile (side view) SHAPE – a curved upper surface and a less curved, or straight, lower one. In other words, a wing must be given some thickness.

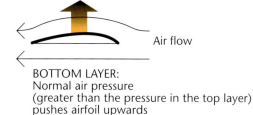

Camber creates lift

TOP LAYER: Speeded up air creates a layer of lowered air pressure

Air flow

BOTTOM LAYER: Normal air pressure (greater than the pressure in the top layer) pushes airfoil upwards

Direction of travel →

It was discovered that a horizontal plane surface with a curved top (CAMBER) has special properties for controlling the speed of air. Why? THE DISTANCE OVER THE TOP IS LONGER than the distance along the bottom. Therefore air flowing over the TOP of the cambered plane has to go further than the air flowing along its BOTTOM. It has to go the long way around the curve while the air underneath can go in a straight line. In order for both streams to meet at the same time at the back edge of the plane surface, the air on top has to "hurry up" to get there. This increase in speed decreases the force of its pressure downward on the horizontal surface. The force of the higher pressure slow-moving air underneath the surface pushes upwards creating LIFT. This is the application of the principle that Bernoulli discovered. It is called AERODYNAMIC LIFT. (At the wingtips, however, air is turbulent because it slips around the tip from the high pressure layer to the low pressure one creating a swirl, called a VORTEX, which produces VORTEX DRAG.) The lifting force is centred along the thickest part of the wing. Any cambered plane surface that creates lift when air flows across it is called an AIRFOIL.

Because air has to move across an airfoil to create the pressure differential, a moving airplane can stay aloft while a motionless one cannot.

THINK AND DO:
- *Collect some bird feathers. What shape do they have?*
- *Repeat the demonstration of Bernoulli's Principle several times. Try it with a feather instead of with paper. What happens?*
- *In your mind, applying the principle to the wing of an airplane, can you see how the curved top of a horizontal plane gives lift?*

Anthony Fokker was trying to find a way of reducing drag by eliminating wire wing braces. So he built the wings around a thick and strong central spar that ran from wingtip to wingtip. To his surprise the wings created much more lift because of the added thickness. The Fokker D VIII shown here was among the first successful airplanes with only one pair of wings and no wire braces. Along with the D VII biplane, it saw service in the First World War.

ANOTHER WAY OF CREATING LIFT

Even an uncurved flat plane surface can become an airfoil. Maybe you have stuck your arm straight out the window of a moving car (a dangerous thing to do) and felt the moving air. If you tilt your hand up even a little, the air tries to lift your arm. It does this because the moving air now strikes the flat palm of your hand and is deflected downwards. In reaction your hand is pushed upwards. By tilting your hand you have given it an ANGLE OF ATTACK. It is the angle at which a plane surface meets the air flow. The greater the angle, the greater the resulting lift.

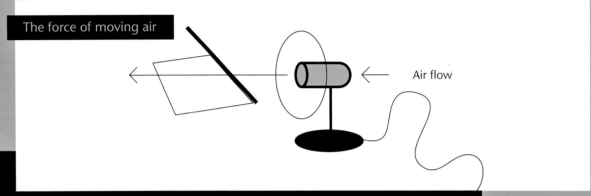

The force of moving air

THINK AND DO:
You can demonstrate the effect of an angle of attack and the force of moving air (without the danger of sticking your arm out of a car window) with a half sheet of ordinary paper and a fan. Tape one short edge of the sheet to a ruler. Holding the ruler horizontally, with the paper hanging down, bring it in front of a fan.

- *Which way does the paper tend to move?*
- *Push down on the free back edge of the paper to create an angle of attack. Can you feel the force of the flowing air pushing against the flat side?*
- *In which direction does the air try to push the paper?*
- *Turn the ruler vertically. Which way does the paper tend to move?*
- *Now push sideways on the free back edge of the paper to create an angle of attack. In which direction does the air now try to push the paper?*

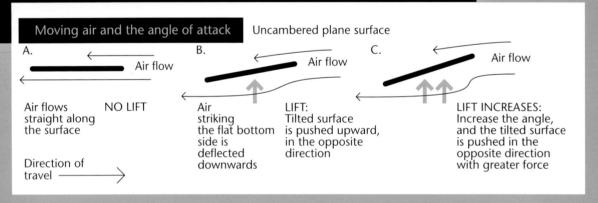

Moving air and the angle of attack — Uncambered plane surface

A. Air flows straight along the surface — NO LIFT. Direction of travel →

B. Air striking the flat bottom side is deflected downwards — LIFT: Tilted surface is pushed upward, in the opposite direction

C. LIFT INCREASES: Increase the angle, and the tilted surface is pushed in the opposite direction with greater force

A flat plane surface with an angle of attack is lifted primarily by the moving air striking the flat bottom side and pushing it upward. But the angle causes the air flowing across the top to travel in a curved manner from front to back, as if the plane surface were slightly curved. A flat plane surface, therefore, also has some aerodynamic lift. Other things being equal, the greater the curvature of its top and the thicker a wing is, the greater its lifting capability. But regardless of camber, an angle of attack increases the lift of any airfoil. An angle of attack is very important for thin wings with slight camber that are found on fast airplanes, like jets. Thick wings for slow-speed flight, like gliding, also make use of the angle of attack. In between are wings of medium thickness designed for moderate speeds, found on many different airplanes. Overall, hundreds of different cambers and thicknesses of wings exist for different kinds of airplanes, and all make use of an angle of attack to increase lift.

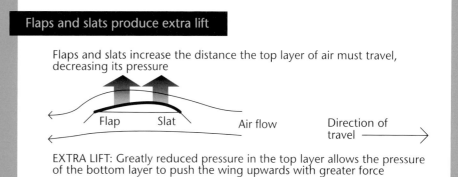

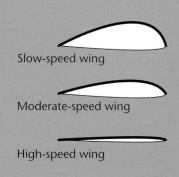

Slow-speed wing

Moderate-speed wing

High-speed wing

THE EFFECTS OF SPEED
An airplane must move forward through the air to create lift. Regardless of camber, as speed increases the amount of lift that any given wing can produce increases greatly. That is why the higher the speed of an airplane, the thinner its wings need to be. At slow speed lift is much less. When airplanes fly slowly two things are done to maintain lift.

First, the angle of attack is increased, which has two effects. It causes the air pressing against the bottom surface to push up with greater force. Also (regardless of camber) as the angle increases, the distance travelled by the top layer of air also increases, lowering its pressure (Bernoulli's Principle). Advantage is taken of both the effects of camber and air pressing against the bottom surface to increase lift.

Second, the camber of the wings is changed. Most airplanes have small surfaces that can be swung down on the trailing edges of their wings. They are called FLAPS. Some airplanes (especially high speed ones with low camber wings) also have surfaces that can be swung down on the leading edges of their wings, called SLATS. When deployed, these surfaces extend the camber of the wings, increasing lift, and make slow-speed wings out of high-speed ones.

DRAG
Lift depends on three things – speed, angle of attack, and camber. All lift has a corresponding penalty of drag. Therefore every increase in either speed, angle of attack, or camber, has some corresponding increase in drag. Unless counteracted by thrust, drag slows an airplane down.

STALL
As the forward speed of an airplane decreases, its nose is pitched up increasing both the angle of attack and lift. But when the angle of attack of most wings is greater than about 15°, lift stops. (Delta wings are more tolerant.) The air flowing over the top surface stops flowing smoothly and becomes very turbulent. This is called a STALL. The airplane keeps moving forward but the wings are ineffective. There is a danger of going into a spin and losing altitude. It is also possible to stall only one wing when making a turn. Stalls are sometimes done at high altitudes by aerobatic pilots as stunts. At low altitudes stalls could prove dangerous because the airplane loses altitude quickly and could crash into the ground.

Moving air gives control

Lift is not enough for an airplane to fly successfully. It must also fly in a straight and level forward motion. It must be stable in the air and its motion must be controllable at all times. An airplane that is hard to control is dangerous.

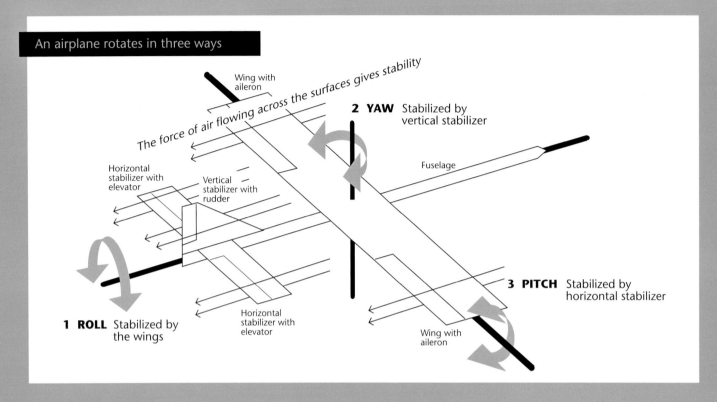

An airplane rotates in three ways

The force of air flowing across the surfaces gives stability

1 **ROLL** Stabilized by the wings
2 **YAW** Stabilized by vertical stabilizer
3 **PITCH** Stabilized by horizontal stabilizer

CONTROL SURFACES

An airplane has both horizontal and vertical flat plane surfaces to give it stability. They are simply called STABILIZERS. In a conventional airplane they are designed as a single unit at the tail end, called the EMPENNAGE. They counteract an airplane's tendency to rotate and wobble in flight. An airplane in flight rotates or pivots in three ways. It:
 1 ROLLS around a line running along its length from front to back.
 2 YAWS around a line running up and down through the middle of the wings and fuselage.
 3 PITCHES around a line running along its wings causing the nose to go up and down.

On the trailing edges of the stabilizers and the wings are small flat plane surfaces that are hinged and movable. They are called CONTROL SURFACES. Their movement gives an airplane three-axis directional control by controlling the rotations listed above as follows:
 1 AILERONS on the wings control roll.
 2 RUDDERS on the vertical stabilizers control yaw.
 3 ELEVATORS on the horizontal stabilizers control pitch.

How do they work? Any flat surface tilted into the flow of air has the same effect as the angle of attack of a wing – it is pushed in the opposite direction from that in which it is slanted. This works on both horizontal and vertical surfaces. As a hinged control surface is moved, the flow of air is disrupted – it is deflected away from the surface of the airplane. This causes the airplane to move in the opposite direction – either rolling, yawing, or pitching, depending on which control surface is moved. For example, moving the rudder to the left causes the tail to move to the right and the nose to go left. This has made the airplane assume a new ATTITUDE. Its nose has moved. Attitude is any change in position, relative to a point on the horizon.

Besides maintaining an airplane's stability in flight it is important to be able to climb, turn, and descend. An airplane must be MANEUVERABLE. In the cockpit of an airplane are a stick or wheel that move the ailerons and elevators, and foot pedals that move the rudder, giving three-axis control. Climbing is done by raising the elevators. The force of moving air pushes the surfaces down, raising the airplane's nose. This slants the wings up into the moving air creating an angle of attack and increasing lift. The airplane rises. The forward speed and the angle of attack must be controlled so that the wings do not stall. Descending is done by reducing thrust. Paper airplanes always lose thrust because they have no engines to counteract drag. Turning an airplane is achieved by rolling and yawing together, like turning the handlebar and leaning your bicycle at the same time. This is done by raising one aileron, lowering the opposite one and turning the rudder at the same time. Turning requires both hand and foot movement.

On the control surfaces are very small secondary control surfaces called TRIM TABS. They are used to aid the pilot in making slight adjustments in airflow to keep the airplane flying straight and level. When air flows so that the airplane flies without rolling, yawing, or pitching, it is said to be in TRIM. All forces from every direction are in equilibrium. Then an airplane is stable and will maintain straight and level flight.

LANDING AND SPECIAL CONTROL SURFACES

The FLAPS and SLATS are special control surfaces located on the airplane's wings. When they are deployed an airplane can fly at a slower speed and yet maintain a sufficient amount of lift. This is especially good for landing (and sometimes for taking off). This slows the airplane down by increasing drag, which is also good for landing. Some airplanes also have SPOILERS or air brakes to increase drag and help in slowing down. Once an airplane has been brought close to the ground for landing the nose is pitched up (a condition known as a FLARE) just before touchdown. Because of the slow speed, instead of climbing, the wings approach stall as the airplane touches down. This near-stall condition keeps the airplane from bouncing back into the air and makes for a smooth landing. The flare is also necessary so that the airplane lands on its main wheels first, not on the small nose wheel.

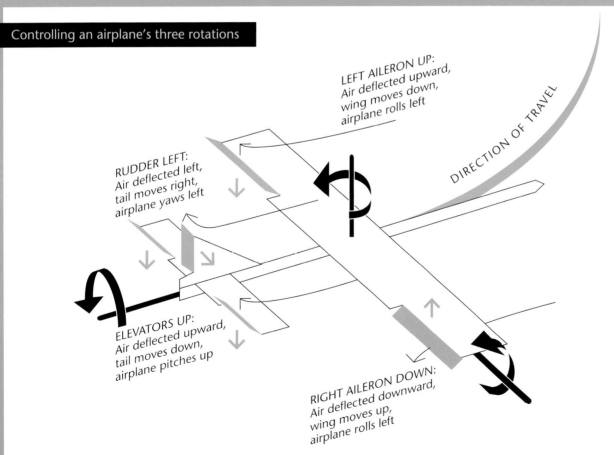

Controlling an airplane's three rotations

With control surfaces in these positions the force of moving air will cause the airplane to turn left and climb

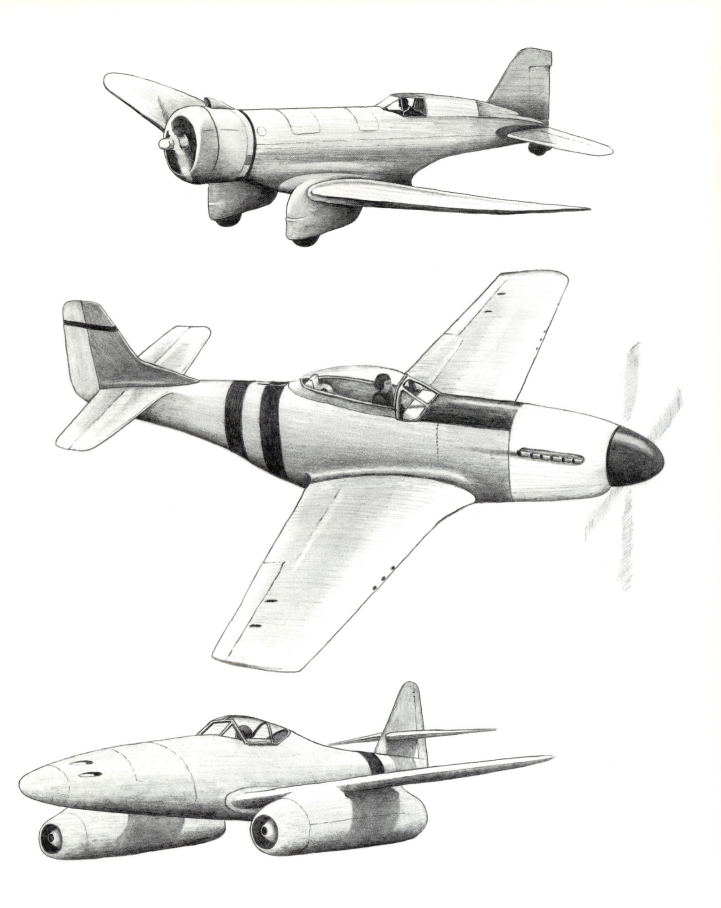

Howard Hughes set a record when he piloted the Northrop Gamma 2G from California to New York in 9 ½ hours at an average speed of almost 300 nautical miles per hour in 1936.

The North American P51 Mustang, designed in 1940 with high speed wings, was a very successful fighter airplane in the Second World War. It went on to set a speed record of over 500 nautical miles per hour.

In 1944, during the Second World War, Germany introduced the first jet-powered airplane, the Messerschmitt ME262. It flew a full 100 nautical miles per hour faster than its closest rival, but it came too late for its superiority as a fighter to change the war's outcome.

Moving air and airplane shape

We can learn about shapes that fly well by looking at birds. In that we are still like our ancient ancestors. There are three main kinds of bird flight. Some birds are strong and steady long-distance flyers, like ducks, geese and swans. Some birds spend a lot of time slowly soaring, like hawks, vultures and eagles. Other birds dart and swoop, like swallows, swifts and nighthawks. Different birds have quite different shapes that help in maneuvering. Like birds, airplanes have different shapes for different kinds of flight.

In the previous two sections we have seen how important profile shape in wings is for flight. But what about other shape factors? We know that airplanes can be made in many different shapes and sizes. When building a new airplane, designers must answer various questions about its use and its shape. If any component is incorrect it will not be a successful flyer. Therefore new airplanes undergo rigorous testing before they are certified as being airworthy. Airplanes can have one pair of wings or two pairs. Some have wings that are attached at the top of the fuselage, and some have wings that are low. Some wings are long, some are short. Some taper, some don't. Some wings stick straight out, others are swept back. Some are narrow, some are wide. Some airplanes are fat and others are thin. Some have round noses and some are pointed. Some can land on water. Some airplanes have one engine, some have none, and some have more than one to fly fast or slow. Each shape is made for a special purpose.

THINK AND DO:
- *Collect pictures of birds in the three flight categories. Put a label on each picture naming the bird and its category of flight.*
- *Look at the shapes of the birds' wings, tails, and bodies. How are they suited to the ways in which the birds fly?*

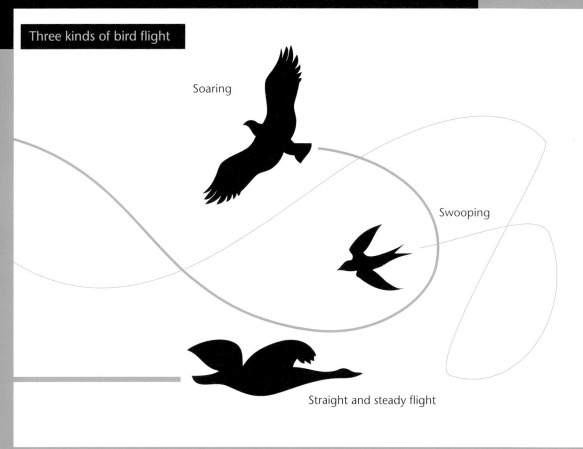

Three kinds of bird flight

Soaring

Swooping

Straight and steady flight

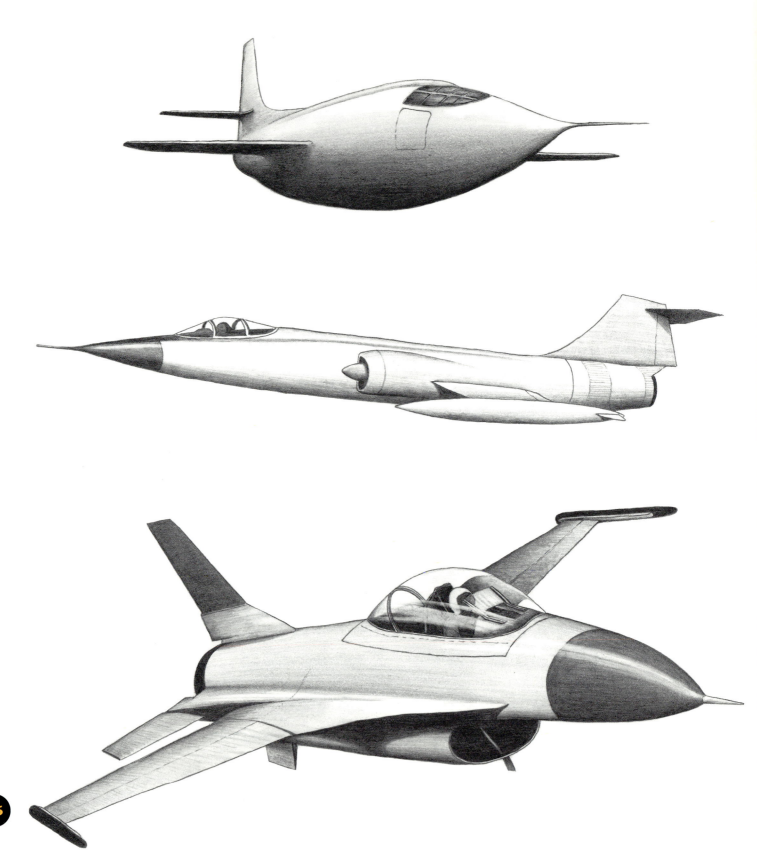

In 1947 Chuck Yeager became the first pilot to fly faster than the speed of sound (about 700 nautical miles per hour). He flew the bullet-shaped Bell X1.

The Lockheed F104 Starfighter was first built in 1954. It set an altitude record of over 39,000 metres in 1963. The next year Jacqueline Cochran set a women's speed record in it at more than twice the speed of sound. For many years it was the all-round highest performing airplane in the world.

The General Dynamics F16 Falcon is one of the most sophisticated and maneuverable fighter airplanes today, having computer-assisted flight and weapons systems, and capable of flying more than twice the speed of sound.

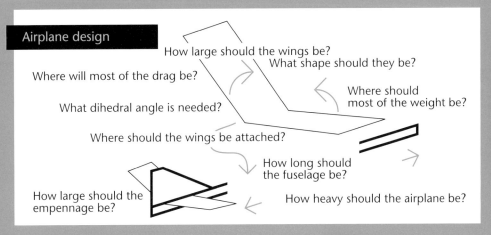

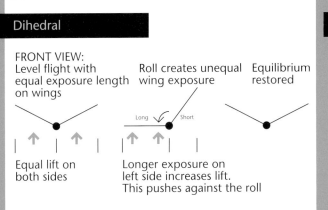

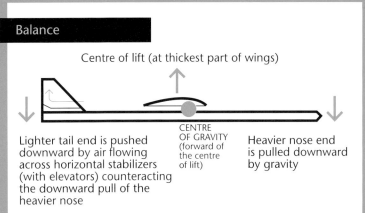

WING LOADING
Although airplanes can be made in many different sizes and shapes they cannot be just any old shape or size. The size of the wings in relation to an airplane's weight is very important. The smaller the wings in relation to an airplane's weight the faster it has to fly to maintain altitude. It is said to have a high WING LOADING. If the wings are too small they will not have enough lift to fly successfully at slow speeds. Large wings in relation to overall weight makes for low wing loading. If wings are too big they have too much drag. An airplane with low wing loading is easily tossed about by turbulent air and can be a dangerous flyer.

DIHEDRAL
To correct the tendency of an airplane to roll in flight the wings and horizontal stabilizers can be attached to the fuselage slanting upward towards the wingtips. This is known as dihedral. When an airplane with dihedral rolls, the lowered wing increases its lifting surface because its exposed length increases, but the raised wing loses some of its lift due to its shortened lift surface, and the airplane returns to level flight (see above). Most airplanes have some dihedral. However, some wings droop down from the fuselage (anhedral). Stabilizers also sometimes slant down.

BALANCE
Even if the above-mentioned factors are correct, the airplane may not fly successfully. Stability also depends on an airplane's balance. Every object has a centre of gravity at which it balances. An airplane's centre of gravity must lie along the fuselage and near the thickest part of the wings, where lift occurs. For greater stability the centre of gravity must lie just ahead of the centre of lift so that in flight the nose end is slightly heavier than the tail end. Then the force of gravity pulls downward at the front of the airplane and it can be trimmed so that air flowing across the horizontal stabilizers (with the elevators) creates a counteracting force at the back to maintain level flight (see above). This action creates TRIM DRAG. If there is too much weight in the front (centre of gravity too far forward), the airplane will tend to pitch downward and nosedive. It will be hard to trim. If the centre of gravity is too far back, it will tend to pitch upward. In both cases, when trimmed for level flight, trim drag will be excessive. The closer the centre of gravity is to the centre of lift, the less stable and more maneuverable the airplane will be.

Whenever an airplane is loaded with passengers or freight, care must be taken not to shift the centre of gravity too much or it may be impossible to bring into trim.

PLAN-FORM SHAPES OF AIRPLANES (top view)

Points on an airplane where the wind resistance (drag) is the greatest is another important consideration in airplane design. It is not possible to build an airplane that has no resistance, but resistance can be reduced. All unnecessary shapes that cause unwanted drag must be avoided. Designing a smooth and clean airplane is called STREAMLINING. But the drag that occurs must be in the right places. It must be distributed so that its force tends to pull the fuselage straight back and keep it pointing forward, like the feathers do on an arrow. It must work in harmony with balance. This is especially important for small engineless craft where ballast is sometimes used to adjust the centre of gravity. Whatever its shape and weight, an airplane must be built so that air can easily flow around it and so that it points forward of its own accord when flown. Together with the size of the vertical stabilizer, this can be built into the plan-form (top view) of an airplane. It needs a thin edge pointing forward to give the least amount of drag at the front and a larger amount of drag (created by the wings and stabilizers) behind the centre of gravity.

Different plan-form shapes, spans of wings, dihedral, degree of camber and wing placement on the fuselage, combine to give different flight characteristics to airplanes. Depending on where the weight distribution is in relation to the drag distribution and the size and shape of its wings and stabilizers, an airplane can be made to be either very stable or very maneuverable. In most airplanes there is a happy medium of stability and maneuverability. Aerobatic and fighter airplanes are highly maneuverable.

Conventional designs have the wings about in the middle of the fuselage with the empennage at the back. Unconventional airplanes have different configurations. The most unusual airplane is the flying wing. It has no fuselage and no stabilizers. The canard has its wings far back along the fuselage with smaller wings near the front. Of all the many different airplanes that have been designed, there are only two basic plan-form shapes. But there are many variations and combinations of the two:

Constant Chord (Straight Wing)
These are good general purpose wings that are more or less the same chord (distance from front to back) along their entire span. They are used for many of the smaller conventional airplanes flying at very slow to moderate speeds.

Delta Wing
These wings are used at a wide range of speeds, from slow to very fast. Delta wing airplanes require no horizontal stabilizers. They can fly at much greater angles of attack before stalling than other wings can.

Variations and Combinations

• **Tapered Wings**
This is a variation on the constant chord wings. They have the least amount of drag and the best glide-and-turn characteristics at moderate-to-fast speeds in conventional airplanes.

• **Swept Wings**
These are variations on the tapered wings (above). They have the least amount of drag and best handling characteristics at high speeds in conventional airplanes. Many jet airplanes use them.

• **Elliptical Wings**
These are wings that are curved along the front and trailing edges. They are variations on taper wings, and fly well at moderate to fast speeds.

Unconventional Features

• **Strake or Chine Wings**
Strake means to lie along. Chine is a word that comes from the word backbone. These are small wings that run along the sides of the fuselage from the nose to the wings. They can be used in combination with any other wing shapes. They allow a wider range of speeds and greater angles of attack in various kinds of airplanes. They act like the small forward wings of the canards or the front portion of delta wings. They also help direct air into jet engines.

• **Winglets**
These are small wings that slant out from the ends of the main wings. At the ends of airfoils the air tends to swirl, creating drag. Winglets use the turbulent air coming off the wingtips and convert it into lift. They increase the main wings' efficiency.

• **Rotary Wings**
This is a special class of airplanes. They have wings that must rotate before they can create enough lift to fly. Each rotor blade is a constant chord wing. If an engine is attached to the rotor (helicopters), they do not need to move forward for taking off. If the rotor is unpowered (autogyros), their flight is just like that of a conventional airplane, except the wings rotate. They need a runway for takeoff.

• **Canard Configuration**
This is another special class of airplanes. The word canard is the French word for duck. The main wings of these airplanes are far back along the fuselage, just like a duck's. At the front is a pair of small secondary wings (called the canards) that act both as airfoils to give lift and as horizontal stabilizers. There are usually no other horizontal stabilizers. The vertical stabilizers are sometimes placed at the tips of the main wings or in the centre along the fuselage.

There are several advantages to this configuration. It is efficient, and able to create a large amount of lift for the resulting amount of drag. It is stallproof. This may be explained as follows. In any airplane, if the nose is pitched up the airspeed drops. Both an increase in pitch and a decrease in speed contribute to stall. A stall does not mean that the airplane stops moving, it means that the wings are not creating lift as they should. In an airplane of conventional configuration a stall means that there is no lift being created and it may go into a dangerous spin. In a canard configuration the small wings are first to stall while the main wings are still providing lift. This causes the nose to drop, increasing speed. As airspeed increases lift is resumed as usual. Therefore a canard is in less danger of going out of control.

The canard configuration is not new to aviation. The first successful powered airplane, the Wright brothers' "Flyer", was a canard. But as different aircraft were designed, the canard configuration was abandoned. In the early days of aviation it was easier to build three-axis control into an airplane when both horizontal and vertical stabilizers were kept together. Therefore building the horizontal and vertical stabilizers as a single unit at the tail end, and placing the wings over the centre of gravity, became standard practice for over seventy years.

This configuration is good but not as efficient as it might be. The stabilizers do not contribute to lift but do add to overall drag. Because they counteract the weight of the nose, they work against lift (see *Balance* on p.17). Canards have their centre of gravity at some point between the two pairs of wings and greater efficiency is attained because all horizontal surfaces are contributing to lift. It results in greater lift for the amount of drag that is created. Among the first of the present-day canards was the Swedish Viggen fighter airplane.

Today efficient flight is very important. Future airplanes must use less fuel and pollute the air less. Airplane designer Burt Rutan has made a number of very efficient canards. His experimental Voyager was able to fly around the world without refuelling. His single seat canards (sold as kits) have become popular. This has sparked a renewed interest in the canard configuration. Paul MacCready's Gossamer Condor is able to fly by being pedalled like a bicycle. Finally the dream of Leonardo da Vinci is possible, but unlike Leonardo's machine, it does not have flapping wings. The Gossamer Penguin is another MacCready airplane. It flies on power obtained from the heat of the sun. Some high speed canards, like the experimental Grumman X-29, depend on computers to fly. Unassisted, the pilot could not make control corrections fast enough to remain in level flight and would lose control. The reason for such an unstable design is to reduce the amount of trim drag and increase the overall performance and efficiency of the airplane.

Together with new lightweight materials and more efficient cleaner-burning engines, canards are the design of things to come. The Beech Starship is one of the first passenger-carrying canards to be brought into service.

THINK AND DO:
Collect pictures of all kinds of airplanes.
- *Can you group them according to the wing plan-form categories?*
- *Compare airplane and bird shapes. Can you find similar characteristics?*
- *Also, can you find pictures showing unconventional characteristics?*
- *Put a label on each picture giving the airplane's name, its use, its wing category, and a short description of why its shape suits its function.*

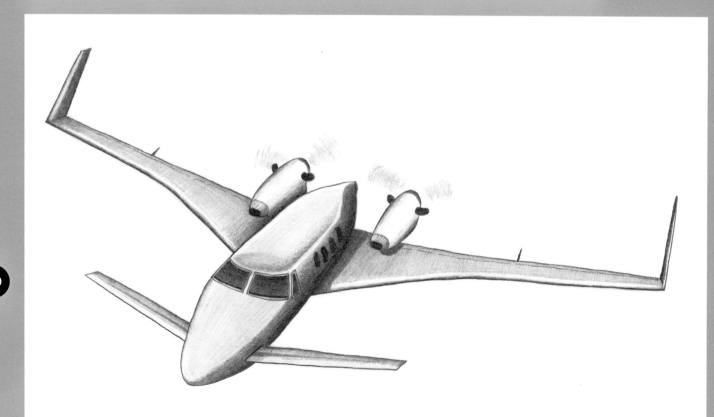

The Beech Starship is among the first passenger airplanes in service having the efficient canard wing configuration.

PART THREE

EXPERIMENTAL FLIGHT

LYING IS WHAT AERODYNAMICS IS ALL ABOUT. Once you know something about the basics of flight and airplane shapes you can build paper airplanes that have controlled flight. In the following experiments you will build airplanes that demonstrate the basic characteristics that every airplane (no matter how large or how fast it goes) needs in order to fly.

Paper is a wonderful material for construction because it can be cut and folded into many shapes and sizes. It is light in weight making it ideal for airplanes. It is readily available. However, paper tends to swell and warp in different weather conditions. The edges of paper airplanes tend to get smashed easily. Therefore they need frequent adjustment and retrimming. Or simply build new ones. This is part of their fun.

Included for experiments 1, 2, and 3, are instructions for making airplanes from plain paper, using tools and materials that are readily at hand. When properly constructed they demonstrate the basic characteristics of the flight and control of airplanes. For experiment 4, reproducible plans of airplanes and instructions for building them are included.

Experiment 1: Principles into practice

Remember that an airplane must be of a shape that tends to point forward of its own accord when it moves through the air. You can demonstrate this with a piece of paper. You will need a sheet of plain paper $8\frac{1}{2}$" x 11", paper clips, cello tape, and scissors. Follow these steps:

1. Cut a sheet of plain $8\frac{1}{2}$" x 11" paper into two $5\frac{1}{2}$" x $8\frac{1}{2}$" pieces. Drop one of them and watch how it moves. Does it go in any particular direction?
2. Add paper clips, one at a time, to one of the narrow sides and observe what happens to its flight? Why? How many clips work best? Can you control its direction by shifting the weight?
3. What shape can you bend, fold, or roll the paper into and fasten with tape, so that when it is dropped it will point forward of its own accord, without extra weight added?
4. Once you have a shape that does, can you find its centre of gravity by balancing it on the tips of your forefinger and thumb? Do you think wings and stabilizers could be added to make it fly? Try adding them, using all or part of your second piece of paper. (Remember, wings must be positioned near the centre of gravity.) If you succeed you have built a rudimentary airplane.

EXPERIMENT 2: Basic controls

With this experiment you begin controlled flight with paper airplanes. This is a common paper airplane, with one difference. It is controllable in flight because you add control surfaces to it.

Follow the instructions to build the airplanes:

Materials
Paper $5\frac{1}{2}$" x $8\frac{1}{2}$" (half sheet of plain copier paper $8\frac{1}{2}$" x 11" – 75 g/m² or 20 lb.)
Cello tape

Tools
Hard pencil (2H or harder) for marking and scoring
Ruler (with steel edge for cutting along)
Craft knife (X-Acto, Olfa, etc.)

> **NOTE ON AIRPLANE CONSTRUCTION:** Remember that all airplanes must be exactly the same shape on each side of the fuselage. It is very important that all of their parts correspond precisely on both sides. Make careful measurements and mark them with a hard pencil. For making sharp folds and bends run a hard pencil along the line with a ruler first to make a score line. Make hinges in the same way. Careful work is important. **Many paper airplanes are poor flyers because of sloppy construction.** Take your time to get things right.

STEP 1: the basic form

SIDE VIEW (Airplane pointing up) TOP VIEW

 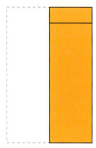    

A. Measure 2 cm at narrow edge and fold over.

B. Fold in half lengthwise with first fold to outside.

C. Fold diagonally from point to outer edge (on both sides).

D. Fold diagonally again.

E. Do it again.

F. Spread the wings.

STEP 2: camber

NOTE: To score a line with a hard pencil, press hard enough to make an indentation in the paper. Be sure to score each fold line.

BOTTOM VIEW

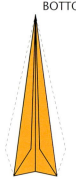 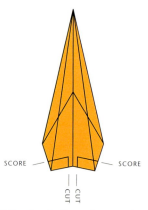

A. Fold the wings as shown.
B. Then unfold them again to finish camber.

C. At the back, 2 cm from outer edge of each wing, cut slits 1.5 cm deep.
D. Score hinges as shown to finish the control surfaces.

STEP 3: vertical stabilizer

SIDE VIEW

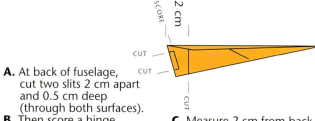 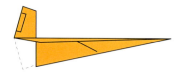

A. At back of fuselage, cut two slits 2 cm apart and 0.5 cm deep (through both surfaces).
B. Then score a hinge between cuts on both sides to finish the control surfaces.

C. Measure 2 cm from back, where wings and fuselage meet. From this point, cut fuselage at right angles to wing surface.

D. Pop up back section to finish the stabilizer. (Note twin rudders.)

STEP 4: finished airplane

SIDE VIEW

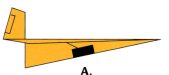

A.
Fasten bottom centre with 2 cm piece of tape.

FRONT VIEW

B.
Adjust for correct fuselage angle, camber, and dihedral angle.

Your finished airplane should look like this.

WARNING: Paper airplanes have sharp points. Never fly them at another person. They could do serious damage to eyes. When flying always establish a flight line that spectators must stay behind.

Test flight:

Every airplane needs to be test flown before it is declared airworthy. This airplane is a delta wing. It is named after the Greek letter of that name, which looks like a triangle. This shape of wing is used in hang gliders as well as in high speed jets, and is a good shape for small-scale paper models as well.

Launch the airplane with a straight-ahead forward motion. Always make the first flight without making any adjustments and observe which way the airplane rotates. (Remember the three rotations.) Then make adjustments deploying control surfaces as needed. Delta wings combine elevators and ailerons in the same controls. Note that this airplane has twin rudders.

Experiment by doing the following:
Always make sure that the airplane is not bent or warped in any way.

1. Fly straight and level – the airplane should not roll, yaw, or pitch but fly straight ahead and descend slowly to the ground.
2. Make turns – by adjusting the appropriate control surfaces (rudder) the airplane should roll and yaw, changing its attitude and its direction of travel.
3. Fly loops – by making the appropriate adjustments (elevators) the airplane should climb steeply, go completely over onto its back, and then continue ahead making a complete loop. Hint: throw airplane up at slight angle.
4. Do rolls – with the correct adjustments (ailerons) the airplane should fly ahead but spin around its longitudinal axis, corkscrew fashion.
5. Does the rudimentary airplane you made in Experiment 1 look anything like this airplane? *Some* characteristics should be similar. Compare the flight characteristics of the two airplanes.

EXPERIMENT 3: Airplane performance

Included for this performance test is an experimental airplane design that is a bit more challenging to build and fly. It too is cut and folded entirely from plain paper.

Notice how wing camber and thickness are made simply by folding the paper. An airplane this light in weight needs only slight wing thickness. Throw this airplane by holding the fuselage from underneath, between thumb and forefinger and just behind the centre of gravity. Launch it with a straight-ahead forward motion. Trim adjustment is a bit more complicated than on the first airplane. Always make the first flight without making any adjustments and observe which way the airplane rotates. (Remember the three ways in which airplanes tend to rotate.) Then make adjustments deploying control surfaces as needed.

This experiment is broken down into a number of test flight exercises to introduce you to the various factors involved in applying aerodynamic principles to airplanes. **You will need to build at least two of these airplanes to complete the experiment.**

Materials
Paper 8½" x 11"
  (plain copier paper 75 g/m² or 20 lb.)
Cello tape

Tools
Hard pencil (2H or harder) for scoring
Ruler (with steel edge for cutting along)
Craft knife (X-Acto, Olfa, etc.)

STEP 1: the airplane parts

NOTE: To score a line with a hard pencil, press hard enough to make an indentation in the paper. Score fold lines to ensure accuracy.

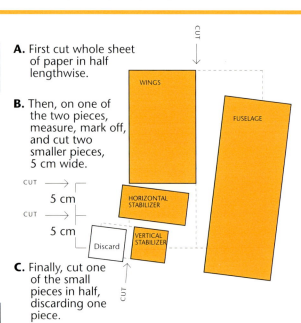

A. First cut whole sheet of paper in half lengthwise.

B. Then, on one of the two pieces, measure, mark off, and cut two smaller pieces, 5 cm wide.

C. Finally, cut one of the small pieces in half, discarding one piece.

STEP 2: empennage (horizontal and vertical stabilizers)

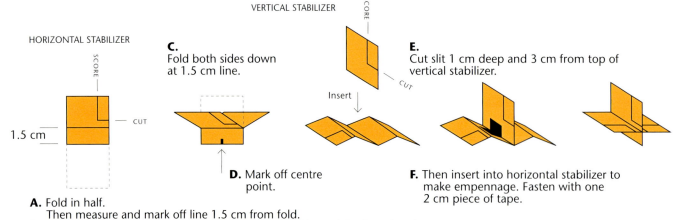

C. Fold both sides down at 1.5 cm line.

D. Mark off centre point.

E. Cut slit 1 cm deep and 3 cm from top of vertical stabilizer.

F. Then insert into horizontal stabilizer to make empennage. Fasten with one 2 cm piece of tape.

A. Fold in half. Then measure and mark off line 1.5 cm from fold.
B. Cut slit 1 cm deep and 3 cm from unfolded edge (through both surfaces). Score hinges on both sides to finish the control surfaces.

STEP 3: wings

A. Fold in half lengthwise.

B. Fold one of the halves in half again, tucking it under.

C. On unfolded edge, cut slit 1 cm deep and 6 cm from each wingtip. Score hinge on both sides to finish control surfaces.

D. Fold in half, then unfold to make a pair of wings.

E. Tape both wingtips, using 2 cm pieces.

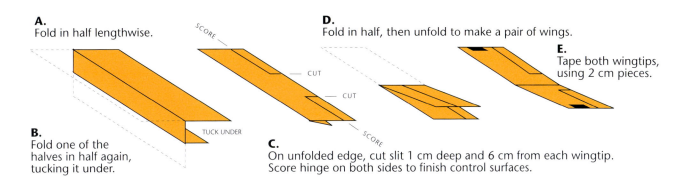

STEP 4: fuselage

A. Fold in half lengthwise, then unfold.

B. Measure 5 cm from one end. Fold over.

C. Fold a point. (Over previous fold.)

D. Fold outside edges in to middle.

E. Fold in half.

F. Fold to outer edge, making flat top.

G. Tape centre top.

H. Measure from back and mark off 3 points.

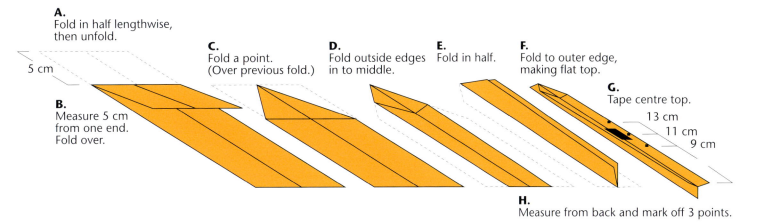

NOTE: Make sure fuselage is not twisted. Adjust fuselage so that front has flat top, and back has dihedral angle.

STEP 5: finished airplane

A. Position front of wings at one of the 3 marks.

B. Insert into fuselage. Align centre mark with back edge of fuselage.

C. Fasten with 2 cm pieces of tape.

FRONT VIEW

D. Correct dihedral angles of wings and horizontal stabilizers.

NOTE: Adjust dihedral together with fuselage top.

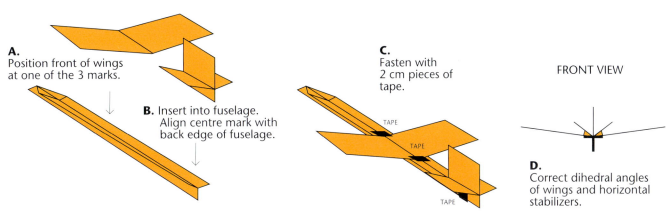

Your finished airplane should look like this.

Test flight 1:
- Attach the wings of one of the experimental airplanes with the front of the wings at the most forward of the three positions marked (13 cm). Find the airplane's centre of gravity by balancing it on the tips of your thumb and forefinger under the wings just where they meet the fuselage. Mark this point on the fuselage CG1. Where is the centre of gravity in relation to the wings' thickest point (centre of lift)?
- Make sure that the elevators are not bent. Throw the airplane. What happens to its pitch?
- Is the balance correct? Do the wings stall? Why?
- Can you adjust the trim to make it fly straight and level?

Test flight 2:
- Carefully remove the wings and reattach them at the most rearward position (9 cm). Again find the centre of gravity. Mark it CG2. Where is it now in relation to the wings? Has it moved?
- Make sure that the elevators are not bent. Throw the airplane. What happens to the pitch now?
- Is the balance correct? Do the wings stall? Why not?
- Can you adjust the trim to make it fly straight and level?

Test flight 3:
- Now attach the wings at the middle position (11 cm). Find the centre of gravity. Mark it CG3.
- Make sure that the elevators are not bent. Throw the airplane. What happens to its pitch?
- Bring it into trim by adjusting the elevators. What have you learned about the relationship between the centre of gravity, lift, and balance? At which wing position is trim easiest? Where should the centre of gravity be for the best flight characteristics?
- Test maneuverability by flying turns, rolls, and loops.

Test flight 4:
- Throw the airplane with its wings pointing up and down (on its side). Does it roll right side up? Why? Bend the wings and stabilizers so they have anhedral. Does it behave differently?

Test flight 5:
- Readjust dihedral. Cut off 2.5 cm of the LEFT WING ONLY. (Tape the cut end.) What happens to its roll and yaw? Why?
- Can you adjust the trim to make it fly straight?
- Cut the right wing to match the left. (Tape the cut end.) Can you adjust the trim to make it fly straight and level? Is the balance good? Hint: Try moving the wings back 1 cm.
- If you haven't already done so, cut and assemble the second experimental airplane. Do NOT shorten the wings. Fly the two airplanes alternately. Compare their airspeeds. Are they different? Why?

Test flight 6:
- Find and mark the centre of gravity on the second airplane. Add weight to the airplane by attaching a small bulldog paper clamp at the centre of gravity. Does the airplane still fly straight and level? What happens to its airspeed? Why? Try this with the cut-wing airplane.
- Try shifting the weight forward or backward off the centre of gravity. Can trim be achieved?

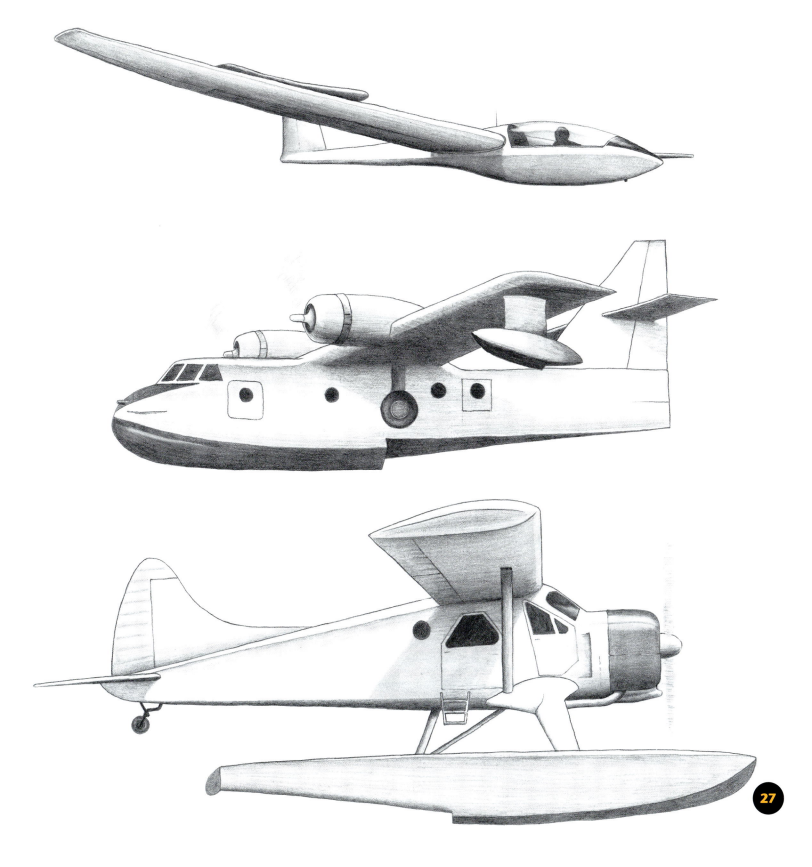

Gliding is a popular sport all over the world. Given the right atmospheric conditions, gliders (also called sailplanes), can remain airborne for many hours. This is the Lark I.S. 28B high performance glider.

Airplanes known as "flying boats" for landing on water have long been built. They were the first to carry passengers across the world's oceans. The Canadair CL215 is amphibious (it can land on water or land). It is used as a water bomber to fight forest fires. Landing on a nearby lake, it can pick up 6 tonnes of water and take off quickly to dump the load where it is needed.

This is a common float airplane in the North. The de Havilland Beaver was first built in 1948 and is commonly used as a "bush plane" bringing people and essential supplies to remote communities.

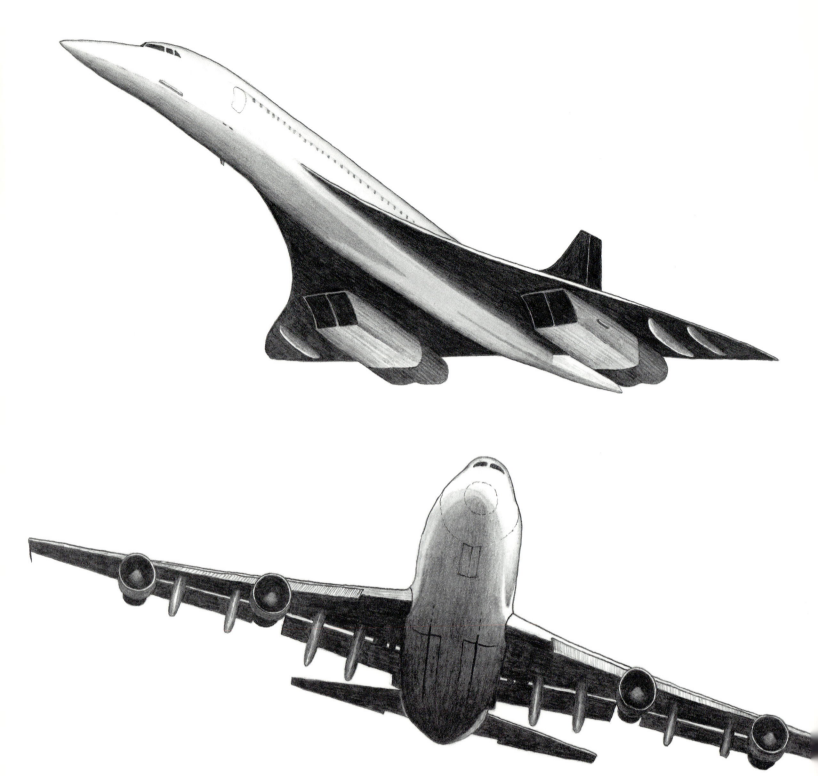

The Aerospatiale Concorde delta wing is today the world's fastest flying passenger airplane, cruising at twice the speed of sound, crossing the ocean from North America to Europe in three hours time.

Among the world's largest airplanes is the Boeing 747, designed in 1969. It is longer than the distance flown by the Wright "Flyer" on its first flight. The 747 can carry 500 passengers plus freight for a gross weight of about 300 tonnes at more than 500 nautical miles per hour. Here it is shown flying slowly with flaps and slats deployed.

EXPERIMENT 4: Competition flying

For this experiment you will have to practice flying until you are an ace pilot. It is an opportunity to show off your flying skills. For added interest, reproducible plans for refined versions of a constant chord, a delta wing, and a canard configuration airplane are included for this experiment. The designs are the results of much test flying to attain proper lift, balance, wing loading, and shape. When *carefully built* they are excellent flyers. These airplanes fly well both indoors and out, but for controlled flight, indoors flying works best. When flying out of doors always fly on a calm day. Out of doors, paper airplanes can fly somewhat further because of wind effect, but with less control over where they will land. They cannot be flown successfully on a windy day.

At school, you could organize teams for this competition and make it a flying event in the gymnasium. If you wish you could set up exhibits about flight and put up suitable decorations.

Carefully cut out the plans found at the back of the book. Photocopy them to build your airplanes, making sure that the image fits **exactly** *on the sheets. Store the originals in a safe place so that you can make new airplanes whenever needed.*

Use the instructions on the following pages to build the airplanes:

Materials
Reproducible plans
   for airplanes, found on pages 41-46
Glue stick & Cello tape

Tools
Hard pencil (2H or harder) for scoring
Ruler (with steel edge for cutting along)
Craft knife (X-Acto, Olfa, etc.)

NOTE: Add colour to your airplanes using felt pens. Broad-tipped highlighters work well. (The ink of some felt pens smears photocopied images.)

How to build the delta wing airplane

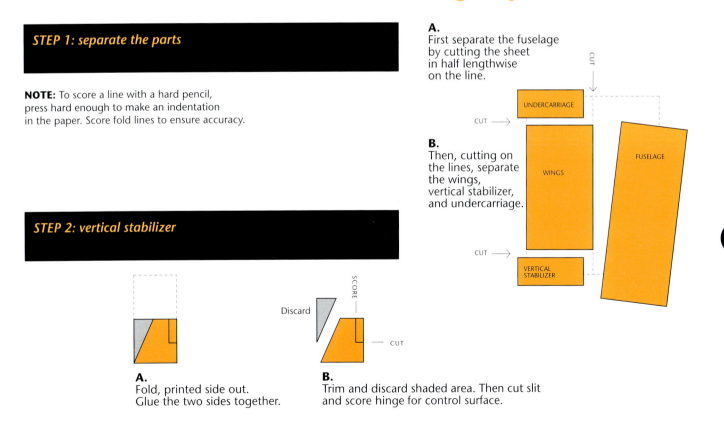

STEP 1: separate the parts

NOTE: To score a line with a hard pencil, press hard enough to make an indentation in the paper. Score fold lines to ensure accuracy.

A.
First separate the fuselage by cutting the sheet in half lengthwise on the line.

B.
Then, cutting on the lines, separate the wings, vertical stabilizer, and undercarriage.

STEP 2: vertical stabilizer

A.
Fold, printed side out.
Glue the two sides together.

B.
Trim and discard shaded area. Then cut slit and score hinge for control surface.

STEP 3: wings

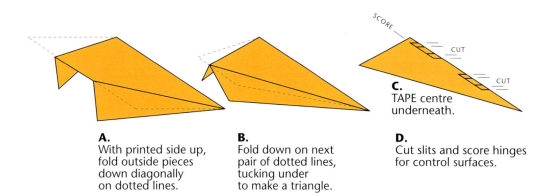

A. With printed side up, fold outside pieces down diagonally on dotted lines.

B. Fold down on next pair of dotted lines, tucking under to make a triangle.

C. TAPE centre underneath.

D. Cut slits and score hinges for control surfaces.

STEP 4: fuselage

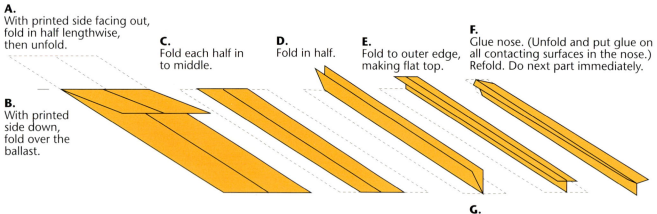

A. With printed side facing out, fold in half lengthwise, then unfold.

B. With printed side down, fold over the ballast.

C. Fold each half in to middle.

D. Fold in half.

E. Fold to outer edge, making flat top.

F. Glue nose. (Unfold and put glue on all contacting surfaces in the nose.) Refold. Do next part immediately.

G. Fold and glue the small triangular points. Do not cut them off. Tuck the centre vertical one in, and the horizontal ones on sides down. Hold until glue sets.

NOTE: Make sure fuselage is not twisted. Adjust so that front has flat top. The back can have slight dihedral.

STEP 5: finished airplane

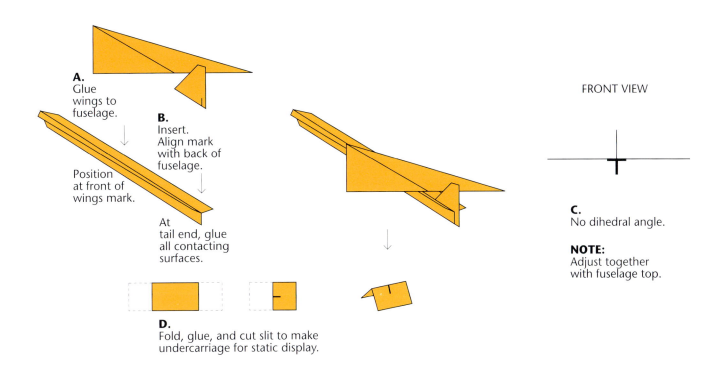

A. Glue wings to fuselage. Position at front of wings mark.

B. Insert. Align mark with back of fuselage. At tail end, glue all contacting surfaces.

D. Fold, glue, and cut slit to make undercarriage for static display.

FRONT VIEW

C. No dihedral angle.

NOTE: Adjust together with fuselage top.

Your finished airplanes should look like this.

How to build the constant chord airplane

STEP 1: separate the parts

NOTE: To score a line with a hard pencil, press hard enough to make an indentation in the paper. Score fold lines to ensure accuracy.

A. First separate the fuselage by cutting the sheet in half lengthwise on the line.

B. Then, cutting on the lines, separate the wings, vertical and horizontal stabilizers, slats, and undercarriage.

STEP 2: empennage (horizontal and vertical stabilizers)

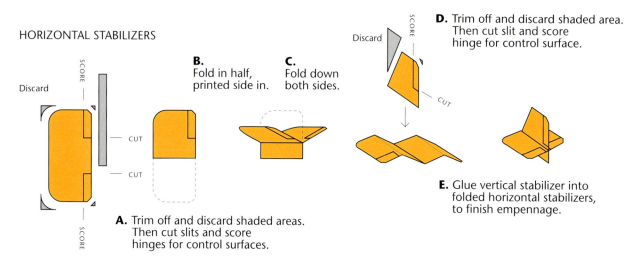

HORIZONTAL STABILIZERS

A. Trim off and discard shaded areas. Then cut slits and score hinges for control surfaces.

B. Fold in half, printed side in.

C. Fold down both sides.

VERTICAL STABILIZER

D. Trim off and discard shaded area. Then cut slit and score hinge for control surface.

E. Glue vertical stabilizer into folded horizontal stabilizers, to finish empennage.

STEP 3: wings

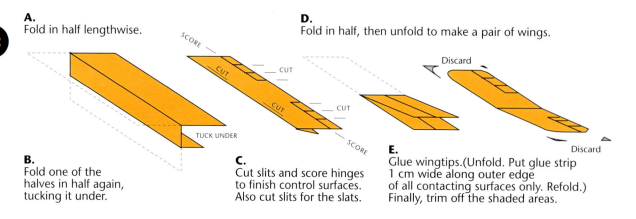

A. Fold in half lengthwise.

B. Fold one of the halves in half again, tucking it under.

C. Cut slits and score hinges to finish control surfaces. Also cut slits for the slats.

D. Fold in half, then unfold to make a pair of wings.

E. Glue wingtips. (Unfold. Put glue strip 1 cm wide along outer edge of all contacting surfaces only. Refold.) Finally, trim off the shaded areas.

STEP 4: fuselage

A. With printed side facing out, fold in half lengthwise, then unfold.

B. With printed side down, fold over the ballast.

C. Fold a point. (Over previous fold.)

D. Fold each half in to middle.

E. Fold in half.

DISCARD

F. Fold to outer edge, making flat top.

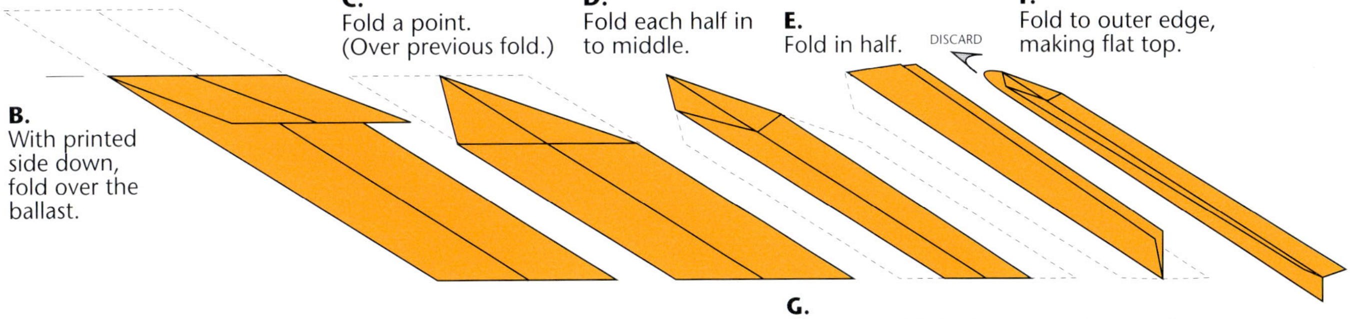

G. Glue nose. (Unfold and put glue on all contacting surfaces in nose.) Refold and hold until glue sets. Finally, trim off the shaded area.

NOTE: Make sure fuselage is not twisted. Adjust fuselage so that front has flat top, and back has dihedral angle.

STEP 5: finished airplane

A. On both pieces, fold slat section down and back section up. (Put aside. The slats are to be inserted into wings to provide extra lift in slow flight. Use only together with flaps and spoilers for landing.)

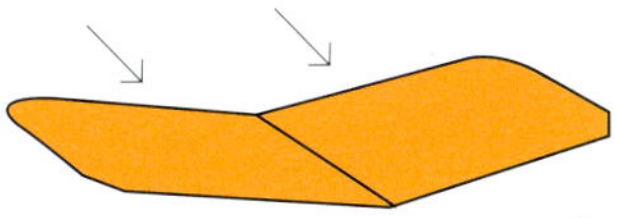

B. Glue wings to fuselage.

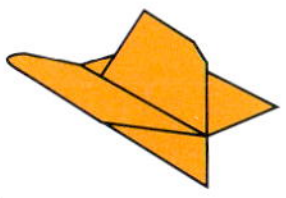

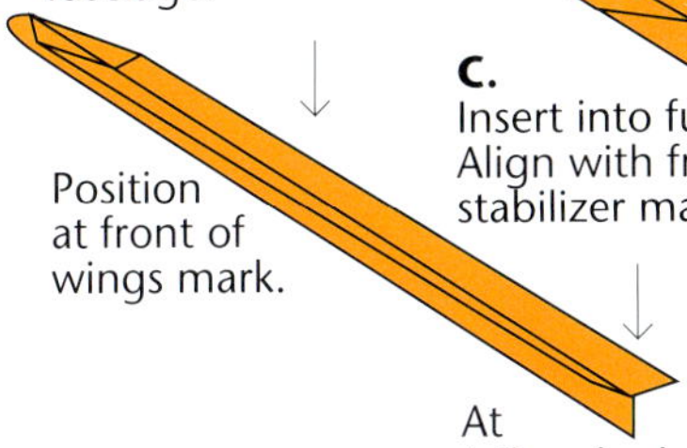

Position at front of wings mark.

C. Insert into fuselage. Align with front of stabilizer mark.

At tail end, glue all contacting surfaces.

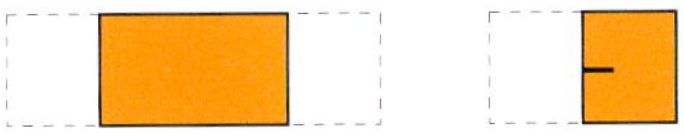

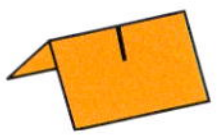

E. Fold, glue, and cut slit to make undercarriage for static display.

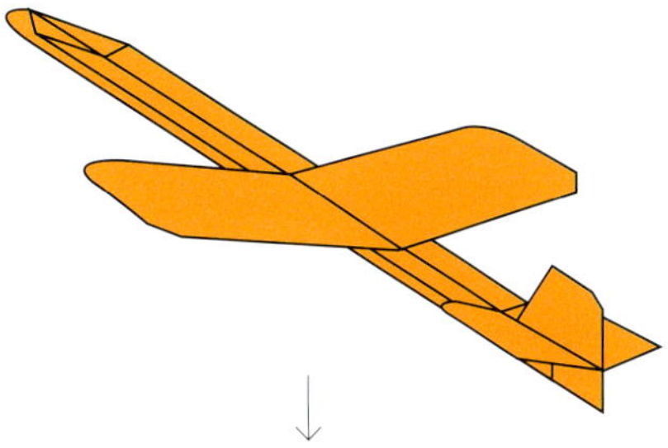

FRONT VIEW

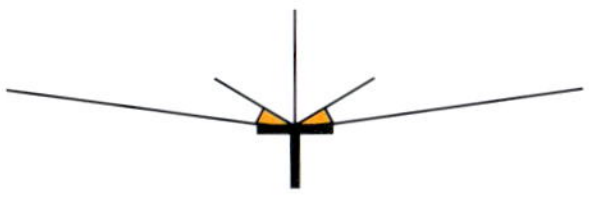

D. Correct dihedral angles: 5° wings, 30° horizontal stabilizers.

NOTE: Adjust together with fuselage top.

How to build the canard configuration airplane

STEP 1: separate the parts

NOTE: To score a line with a hard pencil, press hard enough to make an indentation in the paper. Score fold lines to ensure accuracy.

A. First separate the fuselage by cutting the sheet in half lengthwise on the line.

B. Then, cutting on the lines, separate the wings, vertical stabilizer, and undercarriage.

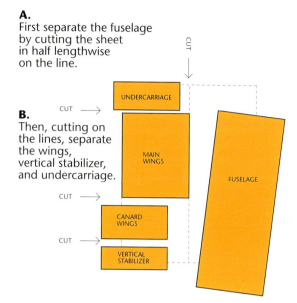

STEP 2: canard wings

A. Trim off and discard shaded areas.

B. Cut slits and score hinges for control surfaces.

C. Fold in half, printed side in.

D. Fold down both sides.

E. Glue base together.

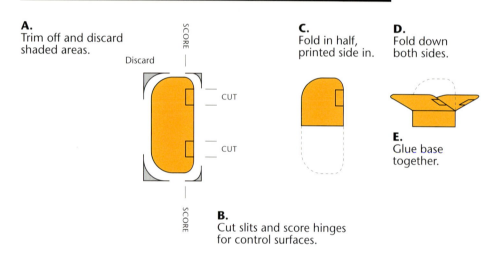

STEP 3: main wings

A. Fold in half lengthwise.

B. Fold one of the halves in half again, tucking it under.

C. Cut slits and score hinges to finish control surfaces.

D. Fold in half, then unfold to make a pair of wings.

E. Glue wingtips. (Unfold. Put glue strip 1 cm wide along outer edge of all contacting surfaces only. Refold.) Finally, trim off the shaded areas.

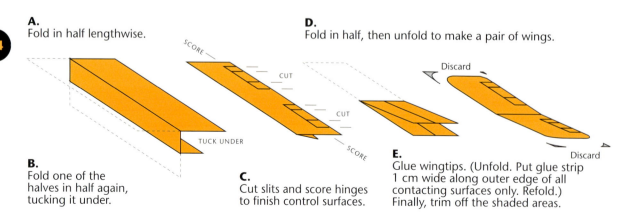

STEP 4: vertical stabilizer

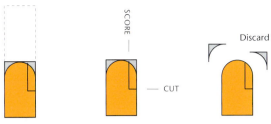

A. Fold over and glue together, printed side out.
B. Then cut slit and score hinge for control surface.
C. Finally, trim off and discard shaded areas.

STEP 5: fuselage

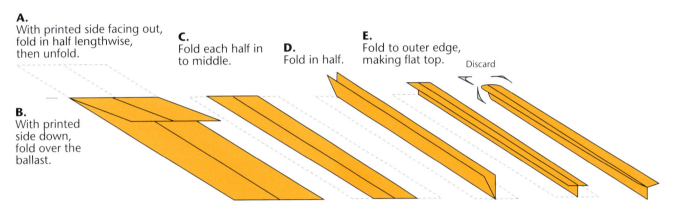

A. With printed side facing out, fold in half lengthwise, then unfold.
B. With printed side down, fold over the ballast.
C. Fold each half in to middle.
D. Fold in half.
E. Fold to outer edge, making flat top.
F. Glue nose. (Unfold and put glue on all contacting surfaces in the nose.) Refold and hold until glue sets.
G. Finally, trim off shaded areas.

NOTE: Make sure fuselage is not twisted. Adjust fuselage so that front has flat top, and back has dihedral angle.

STEP 6: finished airplane

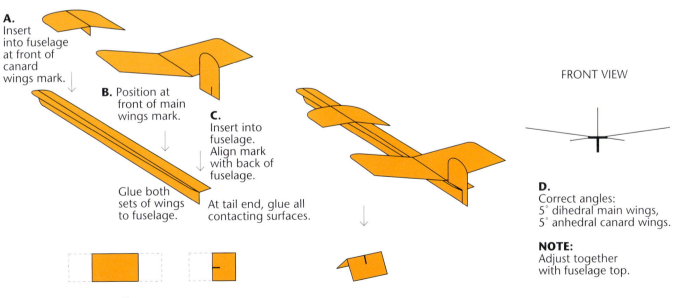

A. Insert into fuselage at front of canard wings mark.
B. Position at front of main wings mark. Glue both sets of wings to fuselage.
C. Insert into fuselage. Align mark with back of fuselage. At tail end, glue all contacting surfaces.
E. Fold, glue, and cut slit to make undercarriage for static display.

FRONT VIEW

D. Correct angles: 5° dihedral main wings, 5° anhedral canard wings.

NOTE: Adjust together with fuselage top.

COMPETITION FLYING

Now you can show off your piloting skills. The objective of the competition is to make three kinds of flights with your airplanes: (a) *fly in straight and level trim* (b) *fly maneuvers* and (c) *make landings.* **Any or all of the three airplanes can be used.** You decide.

> **WARNING: Paper airplanes have sharp points. Never fly them at another person. They could do serious damage to eyes. When flying always establish a flight line that spectators must stay behind.**

Notice that the three kinds of airplanes have different arrangements of control surfaces. On some airplane designs one control surface is required to serve several functions, depending on the speed and maneuver being flown.

Because paper airplanes get out of trim easily and must constantly be retrimmed it often takes several flights in a row to get it right. Therefore it is a good idea to allow each participant to fly more than one flight in each round before giving the turn to the next person. Because control surface hinges wear out quickly, you may wish to build one airplane and leave it trimmed for straight and level flying and build another for maneuvers and landing.

Competition flight 1:
STRAIGHT AND LEVEL – The objective is to adjust your airplane to the best trim and make it fly as far and as straight as possible before touching down.

Mark a starting line on the floor giving yourself lots of space. You could start on a raised surface (like a chair or the gym stage). Mark off one-metre intervals on the floor. Decide on how many rounds you want to fly for the game.

For each round give points as follows:
- Give 5 points for each metre of distance under 8 metres regardless of flight quality.
- Give 10 points for each metre over 8 metres.
- Subtract 20 points for nose-dives or stalls.
- Subtract 10 points for level but not straight.

Competition flight 2:
MANEUVERS – The objective is to deploy the appropriate control surfaces and then regulate the thrust to complete the maneuver.

You must do three maneuvers to complete the round:
- First make your airplane fly a 180° turn before it touches down.
- Then make it fly one complete loop.
- Finally make the airplane fly one or more complete rolls.

For each round give points as follows:
- Give 10 points for each completed turn, loop, or roll.
- Subtract 5 points for incomplete flights.

Competition flight 3:
LANDING – The objective is to make controlled slow-speed landings, with the airplanes having the correct angle of attack. Landing paper airplanes is like playing darts in slow motion, using aim and thrust, and can be lots of fun.

Landing an airplane is the most difficult part of flying. Great skill is required to land any airplane. When an airplane lands it must fly at a slower speed and be gently brought down to the ground. What happens to lift when the speed of air flowing over the wings is decreased? What can be done to compensate for this?

The airplanes should touch down smoothly, not flop down or nose-dive. The objective is to make a controlled slow approach and land the airplanes without stalling too soon or landing on the nose. In a proper landing the wings should stall just at the point of touchdown. The SLOWEST possible speed is important. Do the three airplanes have the same landing speeds? Not only should the touchdown be slow and smooth it should occur *down the centre* of the runway.

DELTA WING:
For landing, deploy spoilers (air brakes) by bending them up 90°. Deploy the flaps by bending them down 90°. This airplane has no slats. For landing, the elevators need to be bent up a little more than for straight flight. Experiment with the angles of all the control surfaces.

CONSTANT CHORD:
For landing this airplane, install the leading edge slats and bend them down 90°. Then slide them in or out until you find the best position (third or fourth mark). Experiment. Also deploy the flaps by bending them down 90°. Deploy the spoilers (air brakes) by bending them up 90°. For landing, the elevators need to be bent up a little more than for straight flight. Experiment with the angles of all the control surfaces.

CANARD:
For landing the Canard, deploy spoilers (air brakes) by bending them up 90°. Deploy the flaps by bending them down 90°. Adjust the elevators. This airplane has no slats. Experiment with the angles of all the control surfaces.

Mark out the runway as shown in the diagram on the following page. (For a simpler one mark only the centre square metre section.)

- For the competition give points as indicated, counting where the airplane *comes to rest*. For disputed positions measure from the airplane's centre of gravity.
- For a poor landing (bellyflop or nose-dive) give only *half* of the indicated points.

FLARE: The angle of attack for landing should be as shown – avoid either too steep or nose-down attitude.

Runway Layout

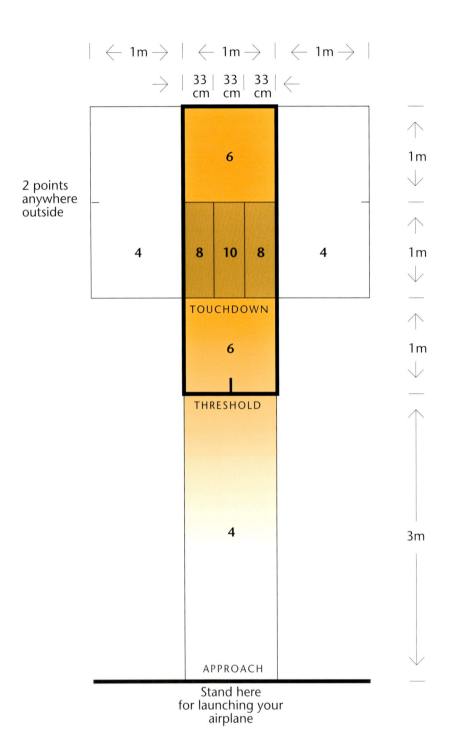

Glossary of terms

Aerodynamics: The study of air as it moves around objects or objects moving through the air.

Aerodynamic lift: Lift created by a pressure differential above and below an airfoil.

Aileron roll: When an airplane rotates around its length as it flies straight ahead.

Airfoil: The wing of an airplane having a flat bottom surface and a curved top surface. When it moves forward air flowing across its top is caused to speed up more than the air on the bottom and becomes lower in pressure (see Bernoulli's Principle).

Air pressure: The force of air pressing on all objects on the face of the earth.

Angle of attack: The downward slant, from front to back, of an airfoil.

Anhedral: The downward tilting of the wings or horizontal stabilizers away from the fuselage making an upside down V-shape when looking from the front.

Attitude: The roll, yaw, or pitch of an airplane, and the direction it is pointing in relative to the horizon.

Bernoulli's Principle: The pressure of a fluid (air) becomes less as its speed increases.

Camber: The curvature of the top of an airfoil (airplane's wing).

Chord: The distance from the leading edge (front) to the trailing edge (back) of a wing.

Control surfaces: Small flat movable surfaces that are used to maneuver an airplane in flight. They are:

- **Elevators:** Surfaces on the horizontal stabilizers that control pitch.

- **Ailerons:** Surfaces on the trailing edges of the wings that control roll.

- **Rudder:** Surfaces on the vertical stabilizers that control yaw.

- **Flaps:** Surfaces on the trailing edges of the wings that increase lift and increase drag.

- **Slats:** Secondary flaps on the leading edges of the wings that increase their lifting force.

- **Trim tabs:** Very small control surfaces that make it easier for the pilot to keep an airplane flying straight and level.

- **Spoilers:** Air brakes. Flat surfaces that can be moved so that they stick out to create enough drag to quickly slow down the airplane or to reduce lift. They are located on the wings or the fuselage.

    NOTE: On some airplanes (especially delta wings and canards) the functions of some control surfaces are combined (for example, elevators and ailerons). The same control surface can be used to achieve different results, depending on the maneuver being flown.

Dihedral: The upward tilting of the wings or horizontal stabilizer away from the fuselage making a V-shape when looking from the front.

Drag: The force of wind resistance tugging on moving objects that slows them down.

Empennage: The tail. The horizontal stabilizer and the vertical stabilizer designed as a single unit at the tail end of an airplane.

Flare: Pitching the nose up during landing just before touchdown on the runway.

Fuselage: The body of an airplane. The wings and stabilizers are attached to it.

Gravity: The force of the earth on all objects (including airplanes) that pulls them to the ground and gives them weight.

Lift: The rising force that is created when lower air pressure above an airfoil allows the air with higher pressure underneath it to push upward (aerodynamic lift). Lift is also caused by the deflection of air striking the lower surface of an airfoil with an angle of attack, pushing it upward.

Maneuver: Skilfully making an airplane move in the correct manner and fly in the desired direction.

Pitch: The rotation of an airplane around a line running widthwise through its middle causing the nose to go up or down.

Plan view: The view of an airplane looking from the top.

Roll: The rotation of an airplane around its length causing the wingtips to rise or fall.

Profile view: The view of an airplane looking from the side.

Stabilizer: A flat surface on an airplane that directs the flow of air, keeping it moving straight and level.

Stall: The condition that occurs when a wing is tilted up at the front (about 15° for most wings), and air flowing over its top becomes turbulent, causing lift to stop.

Streamlining: Making an airplane's shape so smooth or "clean" that air flows across it with the least amount of drag possible.

Thrust: The force needed to push an airplane forward to overcome drag.

Trim: The condition of forward motion when air is directed across all the control surfaces so that an airplane does not roll, pitch, or yaw.

Trim drag: The drag produced when trimming an airplane.

Vortex: Air that slips off the wingtips from the high pressure zone to the low pressure zone on either side of an airfoil, and swirls in a circular manner behind each wingtip.

Vortex drag: Drag produced by the vortex. Every airfoil produces it.

Wing loading: The amount of weight a given area of wing is required to lift.

Wing span: The distance from wingtip to wingtip.

Yaw: The rotation of an airplane around a line from top to bottom through its middle causing the nose to go left or right.

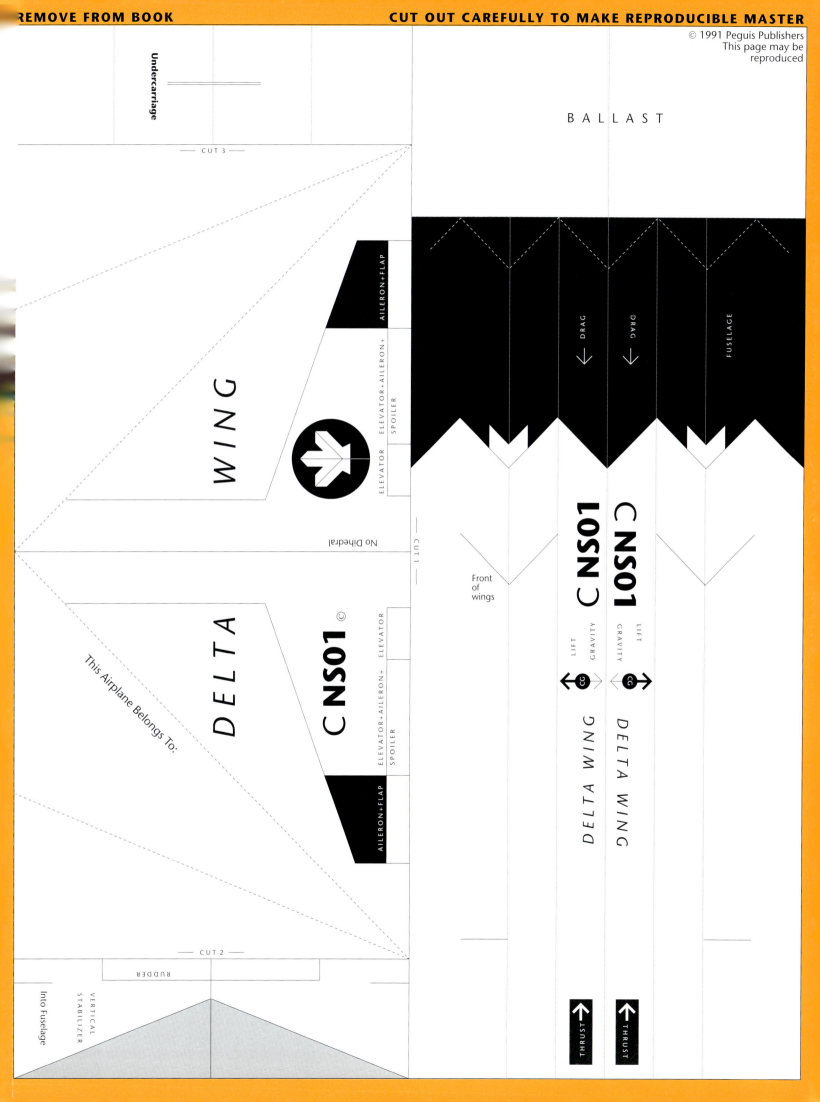

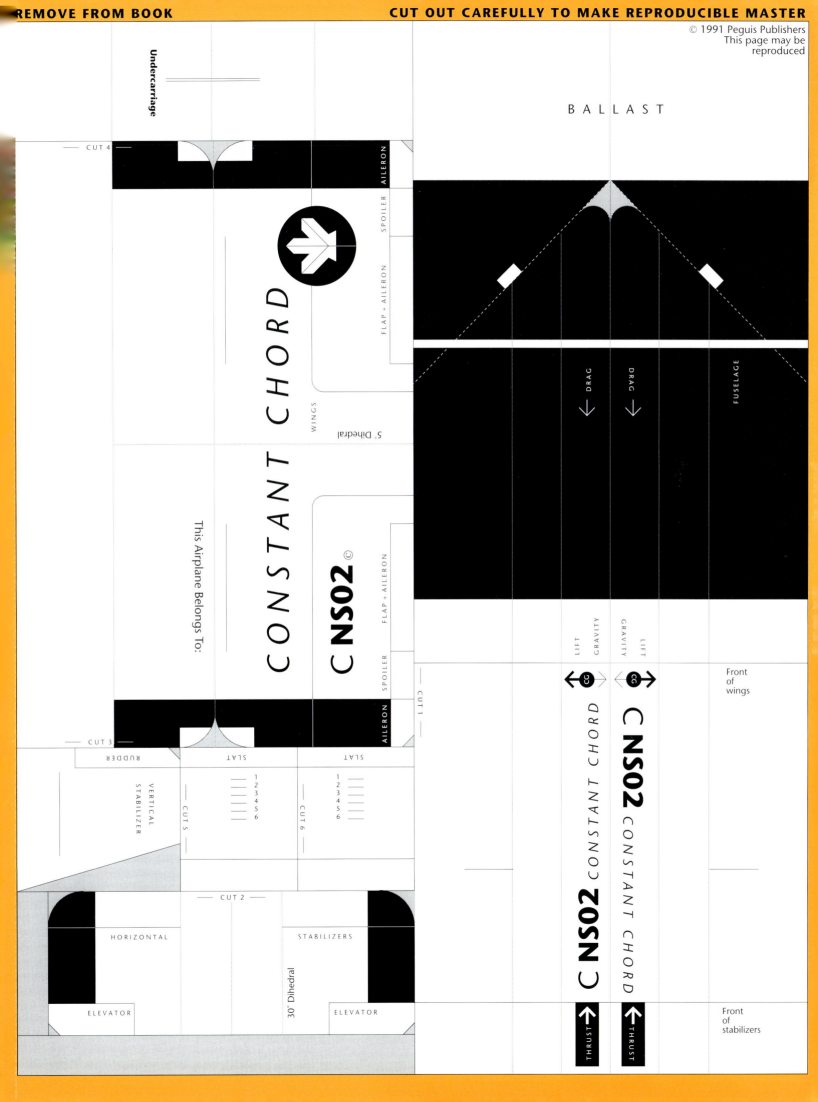

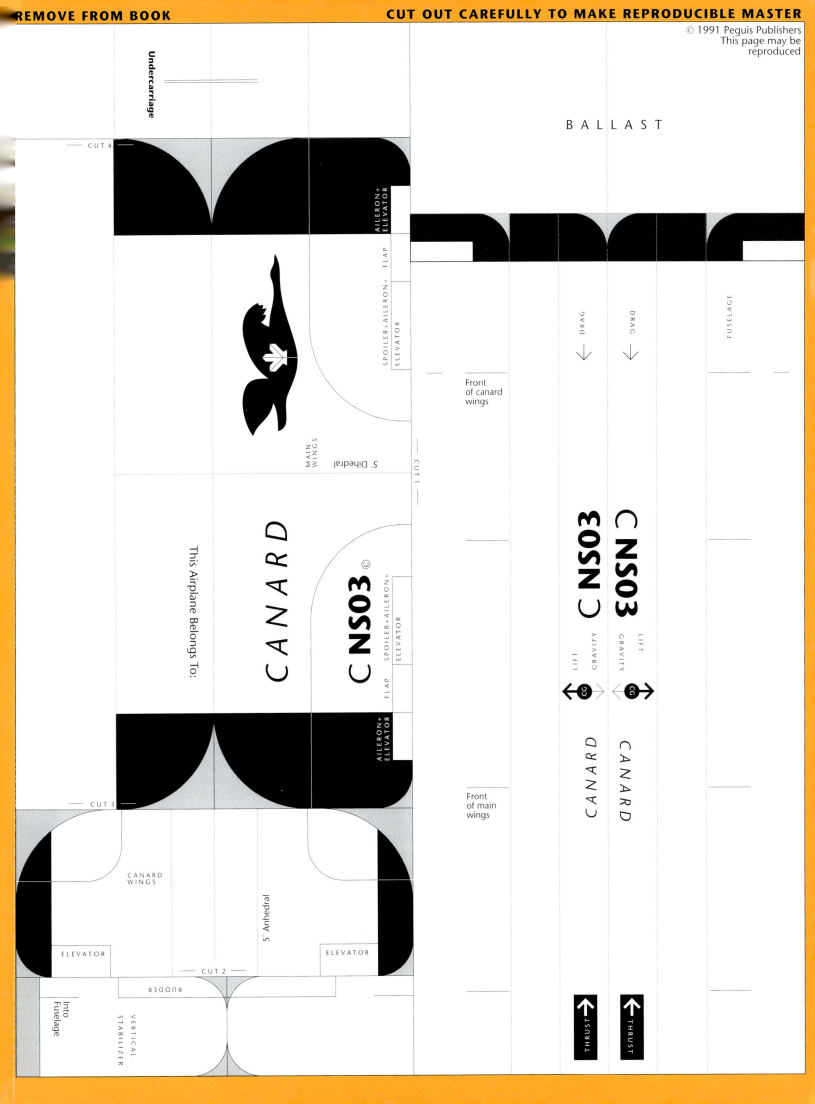